Graphics by Rachael Vines

gpearlpublishing@gmail.com

ISBN# 9798329026917

PUBLISHING LLC.

Dedication

This book is dedicated to all those who suffer unjustly and those who have taken up the fight for social justice issues and better race relations.

The Hand that Rocks the Cradle:

A Treatise on Social Justice and Race Relations

Introduction

Social justice and race relations are really important issues in today's society. There are a lot of good people who can't believe what is happening when it comes to these issues, nor can they fully understand what is happening. This book has been written to explain these very delicate and highly explosive issues by exposing the hidden hand that is, in many instances fomenting, controlling, and/or ignoring what is going on in society.

Any person who is in a position to share information on societal issues is duty-bound and has a responsibility to express the truth as they know it, without using any artificial sweeteners or deceptiveness. This should be done no matter who agrees or disagrees with the truth. No matter how much discomfort it brings. Or no matter how popular or in vogue something is or isn't. None of that should matter, but the sad fact is, that all of that seems to matter. This is why truth has become stranger than fiction.

Those who control the media news outlets control what is or what is not reported. And if something is put before the people that are highly controversial or would reveal something they don't want to be made known, it has to be preapproved. And if it is preapproved, it is given a certain slant to fit a particular narrative.

Media giants and those who have powerful political platforms use propaganda as their chief tool to steer the thinking of the people by coloring the people's perceptions. This seeds the subconscious mind. This is important to point out because when you come up with a thought, an idea, or a viewpoint that you think is exclusively yours, it is not, it has been greatly influenced by powerful masters of psychology who understand the power of the subconscious mind and how it can bring up things previously placed there over time and under the right circumstances.

Many of the seemingly varying views that come from people from across all platforms contain the same genetic material as the original thought those views came from. The framework of this society will not give the people the ability to think beyond the parameters of what is prescribed to them through its institutions. This enables powerful rulers and elites to exercise their dominance and control in such a way as to predict outcomes and responses with great ease and accuracy.

None of what you are witnessing or going through when it comes to social justice issues or race-related issues is by accident. Real conditions come from real places. If the effect of something is real, then the cause that produced it is just as real. Generally, effects are seen, but causes are not. You can't get something out of nothing. To do so would defy the laws of mathematics, the laws of physics, and the laws of logic.

The Hand that Rocks the Cradle will take you into the understanding of how systemic racism and governmental agencies control many of the events plaguing black, brown, and white communities. Their controlling influence causes the activity that is going on in this nation and world to reflect their aims. This book is not conspiratorial by nature. Yet for certain plans to be effective, people have to conspire and agree to engage in actions that facilitate their agenda.

This book is not to play the blame game, make excuses, or point fingers. It is to explain the reasons why this or that is the way it is. The only thing asked of you is that you reason with what is being presented in this book. My plan is to point out with great clarity what I believe to be the root cause of much of the commotion in the world as it pertains to social justice and race-related issues. Attempts will even be made to offer basic solutions that will help in curbing the effects of the extended abuses suffered by many blacks, browns, and even many whites in this country.

Be forewarned, the contents of this book are rough, abrasive, and coarse. When blacks and whites are mentioned in certain instances, it's not referring to every black person or every white person. I know that I can't paint everything or everyone with a broad brush. However, I will hold nothing back in offering my critical critique of what I see being played out daily in this country that supposedly is founded with certain freedoms in mind. Freedoms that many in this country have never experienced because they were never intended for everyone.

The founding fathers did not envision an America that would become the melting pot that she is today. If America is to survive as a Nation, then she must evolve and shed off her old ways, repent, and do right by her citizens and the citizens of the world who are affected by America's policies. But greed, wickedness, and world dominance supplant any ability to have any compassion for those who are crushed under America's foot by her selfishness, greed, and blinding ambition.

This book will be very critical of both blacks and whites and won't cater to people's sensitivities. Holding back won't allow us to go forward. If this problem between the races is handled properly, it will be painful for many, but in the end, things will be better off. Sometimes it takes being made uncomfortable. It takes speaking truth to power. It takes being able to withstand the judgments of others who disagree with you. And above all, it takes great strength to speak while being unafraid of consequences or censorship.

In this book, beliefs will be challenged, attitudes will be exposed, and knowledge will be tested. I pray that we come out on the other end of this book with a broader perspective and understanding of certain aspects of social justice and race-related issues. The hand that rocks the cradle has always ruled the world. Let's see who has been rocking the cradle. In doing so, it will expose those who are most responsible for much of the social chaos and bad race relations America and other nations are experiencing.

Terry Triggs

1_ From the Cradle to the Grave

The very moment a black child is born in America, the child is force-fed into a system that intends to shred them into a fraction of their true selves. Inferior education, family dysfunction, inadequate healthcare, crime-ridden neighborhoods, the proliferation of drugs, gentrification, exposure to violence, and teenage pregnancy are all factors that thwart the potential for blacks to succeed. For us to make it in America's society, we must overcome nutritionally deficient and poor-quality food, poverty, racial discrimination, mass incarceration, voter suppression, predatory lending practices, joblessness, and a plethora of other things that are natural obstacles. Because of these realities, many blacks find themselves always treading water.

Aside from favorable circumstances and good old hard work, if you are successful, that often means you slipped through the cracks. You have beaten the odds. Due to the system design to swallow you whole, and if by chance you are one of the few who haven't directly fallen victim, you, by that system, will indirectly have other obstacles and hurdles that you will struggle to overcome. It is unambiguous that there is a segment of white

America that sees a black person's skin as their sin. In their eyes, your only guilt is that you are born black. Many of these same whites who think like this see their white skin color as a badge of honor.

All white people don't see it like this, but many do. Is this the truth, or is this a lie? Part of your perspective of the race issue exists from either your acceptance or denial of this statement. America is at a serious crossroads. Race relations between blacks and whites have always been an issue since the inception of this Nation. I am not mentioning anything that is not already known. We will delve as deeply as we can to shed some light and, more importantly, offer some possible solutions to the race problem that does not seem to be going anywhere anytime soon.

I fear that if nothing meaningful happens to stop the injustice that is a part of the backdrop of America, then this country may be headed for civil war. These two sides, black and white, can't seem to get along in the broadest sense. There is something inherently wrong that needs addressing. If you are rational and objective and go outside of your bubbled existence, you won't be able to deny this fact. On May 25, 2020, in Minneapolis, Minnesota, there was the death of yet another unarmed black man, George Floyd. He was mercilessly murdered at the hands of four white police officers. In the wake of that unjustifiable killing, protests sprung up in several major U.S. cities across America.

The news reporters' conversation in the media primarily turned from speaking candidly about the root causes of this seemingly unending series of deaths of black folks at the hands of white police officers to the types and styles of protests. Branding some protesters as rioters, thugs, and hoodlums. I heard several news commentators speak about how some protesters complained about the focus taken away from George Floyd's death and the justice that his family so desperately sought. In one respect, I agree, and in another, I humbly and respectfully disagree. Listen, if you examine all of the homicides committed by the police against unarmed blacks, you will notice that following each murder, there were protests.

Did anything change for the better? No. Did the killings stop? No. What were the results after each protest? More killings. Was anyone held accountable? Very rarely. Was each killing determined to be justifiable? For the most part, yes. So, when one method of doing something does not work, it is natural to try other methods until you find something more effective. Here we are yelling at the top of our lungs on the rooftop, and those within earshot act like they don't hear all of the clamoring. Our cries for justice have always landed on deaf ears.

Let me ask you something: Do you really think that if this country wanted to make the necessary changes to bring a semblance of peace by administering justice, it couldn't do it? If the government brought every available resource to bear on this national crisis, it can be done with the snap of some very powerful fingers. The race issue should be considered a state of emergency. And because it is not, it should be taken more seriously. Do you mean to tell me that America has all the expertise and financial backing of the world to send Perseverance to roam on Mars, but she can't figure out a viable solution to the explosive race problem right here on Earth?

There exists a solution to every problem no matter how complex the problem is. Where there is a will, there is a way. Since the way is well within your power, I conclude you don't have the will to do it. In later chapters, we will discuss how America profits more by keeping the masses ignorant. We can't afford to sit around and wait for someone else to give us the justice we seek. So, when I see more aggressive protests, I understand. Lines have long been crossed. Boiling points have long been reached. And now, the people are refusing to take it anymore, so their protests evolve to get a different result.

When whatever you do gets the response or result you want, even if you used extremes, then what you did was effective. When someone is not on the other end of injustice, on the other end of an illegal chokehold, or the other end of a knee to the neck, then they have no right to tell anyone in that situation how to respond. Anyone who does that has a hell of a nerve! The powers that be allow for and condone peaceful protests against their violent actions. Sounds ludicrous, doesn't it? Well, it is.

Black people's voices have always yelled the loudest and heard the least. Pray. Sit in. March. Protest. Just stay within the bounds of what is deemed permissible and acceptable, and you'll be just fine. You become a problem if you do or say anything they don't sanction, then you become a problem. Stay passive and docile. But don't rock the boat too much, or they will do everything they can to throw you overboard. They feel comfortable taking this position because, in their eyes, you will always be a slave. A nobody. From the cradle to the Grave.

I wrote this book from inside a prison cell. At the date of this writing, it has been over thirty-one years I have been incarcerated. Therefore, I have a firsthand account of something that most don't. For example, I know emphatically how biased and unfair the criminal justice system is. I am a product of the school-to-prison pipeline, as were and are so many others. Those in prison are at the bottom of the barrel. At the bottom is where all the crap is. The scraps. The worthless stuff. So don't let it be any wonder to you why my words are fashioned the way they are. It is dark at the bottom, and darkness has a way of turning you into itself. Although I am way down here, I keep my head up. And in looking up, I see a smidge of light, which in turn gives me and those similarly situated a glimmer of hope.

Of all the subjects to broach with someone, none are more explosive than race, religion, and politics. I am not oblivious to how what I say may be perceived and the controversy that will surround much of it. I didn't have the fortunate experience of having a "fine" college education to teach me how to articulate myself in a way that is deemed appropriate. So, you might have to excuse my uncouthness. My intentions are not to berate or belittle anyone, but it is sad to me to see how much milquetoast talk people engage in on one side of the race issue and how so much lying, deception, and evasiveness goes on the other side.

I don't know how to tippytoe around this issue. My words travel in a straight line. People want transparency, and that is exactly what they will get in this book. Now, let's get back to these protests.

The root cause of the varied protests stems from injustice, real or imagined. This Nation's system of justice is flawed. This, in turn, poisons the minds of both whites and blacks. Making the former feel like they are better and superior, and the latter feel they are less than and more inferior. This dynamic is played out daily and practically in every encounter between the two.

And this is what Colin Kaepernick was kneeling for. This caused him to pay a very high price to stand for a cause he firmly believed in. A cause much more significant than himself. Look at how he protested. It was peaceful. And even that was mischaracterized as something other than what it really was. This is the deception that I was referring to. They misdirect and change the narrative to fit something that sparks more controversy instead of looking at the real reason why this man took the stand he did.

Why do you do this America? Because you have no concern for the truth. You have no desire to right your wrongs. So, you use your massive media platforms to inundate the airwaves with your fallacies and your character assassinations. This is what you devolved into with Mr. George Floyd. You are more concerned with whether or not he had some illegal substance in his system, as if that trumps or justifies his murder. Right is right, and wrong is wrong. Fess up so we can move forward in a more harmonious way. The truth will set you free. Isn't this what you teach? But you don't believe it, do you? Because if you did, you would free yourself from the weight of your prior evil acts.

But you refuse to acknowledge your wrongs. And if you don't acknowledge your wrongs, then you will do nothing to repair the damage that was done by your racial hatred against people who have been made too divided, too ignorant, and too weak to defend themselves. You should know how the story ends with bullies. It ends the same way every time. I'm not saying that peaceful protests can't yield results. They can, sometimes. Peaceful protest is what a mature and responsible person does to shine a light on issues that need attention to affect some kind of change.

Peaceful protest is the approach Colin Kaepernick took. He peacefully protested, and you detracted from his ultimate aim for protesting. Your line of reasoning is busted up when you say that aggressive or violent protests detract from what the protesters are protesting for. I would argue that any protest that anyone engages in that you don't like or agree with is responded to by whatever method you see fit. Peaceful or otherwise. And this is why when someone exercises their constitutional right to peacefully assemble to protest, they are still penalized, maligned, and castigated.

You will find a way to twist and turn any circumstance to fit your false narratives to sway the thinking of the masses, who are already preconditioned to swallow what you say without questioning it. In no way am I advocating violence. I'm an advocate of justice for all. Unfortunately, sometimes, people listen better when they are confronted with more aggressive tactics. Bullies don't stop bullying all on their own. They will punk you for as long as you let them. You must stand up to a bully with strength. And the real strength is in the power of our collective unity.

So, if one method of protesting has proven not to work, to keep using that same method is idiotic, counterproductive, and a waste of your time, energy and resources. When trying to produce meaningful change, you utilize whatever means are at your disposal to achieve the results you want. Just suppose you go into a dark room and switch on the lights. What would be the natural function of light? To dispel the darkness, right? But what if the natural function of light does not do what it is supposed to do? Shouldn't you resort to other methods to dispel that darkness?

What am I saying? We have voted. We have marched. We protested. Change is happening but at a snail's pace. This change is taking place mainly in the hearts and minds of the younger generation, who don't think like many of the older generation. Ironically, a few years after Colin Kaepernick took his stand that cost him his pro football career, Roger Goodell, the NFL commissioner, admitted that he should have stood by Colin Kaepernick. What I find hypocritical about this is the fact that it had to take other voices and corporations to chime in to make it safe for Mr. Goodell to rear his head and say what he did.

This same climate had all kinds of folks coming out of the woodwork. Can I tell you what I was thinking when this chorus of voices began to sound off after being silent just a few short days before about what has been happening for centuries? I thought, hmm, how convenient. I know people have their careers to think about. Their families. And to speak out would put a huge target on their backs. Fear is a weapon. It immobilizes. Fear is used to keep people who know what is happening from speaking up for what they know is right. Or they are now in different socioeconomic circles that wouldn't be as accepting of their actual views on the issue of race. All of this is rooted in fear.

Emotionalism is never a good tactical response to deal with a rational attack. You can't just fly off the handle. Wisdom has to be used to forge a way forward. If that is your approach, fine. But if your silence is because you don't want to be seen in a particular light by your family, friends, or colleagues, then fear is tied to your decision to remain sidelined no matter what you say. Even when the atmosphere made it safe to speak up, "they", some of "them", spoke so mildly, so politically correct, and danced all around the issue. They did this even as they admitted the direness of the situation. You can't have a situation that is a state of emergency and be all gentle. Never bring a knife to a gunfight. Please don't mischaracterize this statement.

There are a lot of good and well-educated black folks who are very well versed with the history of this Nation with regards to her evil treatment against blacks. That being said, the law of physics clearly states that an object at rest or in motion will remain at rest or in motion unless acted upon by a force equal to or greater than the force causing the object to move or that which holds it in place. What does this mean? It means you have to at least match this onslaught by the enemy with wisdom equal to his or greater wisdom to get up under this thing.

If I have to define 'enemy' then we are in more trouble than I thought. And if I have to justify this terminology, then we will be in even worse trouble.

How would you describe someone who willfully, consciously, and systematically deprives you of the essentials of life? Someone who beats and kills you? Who purposely lies to you? Deceives you? Are those the actions of someone for you or in opposition to you? They are the actions of an enemy. You have to call it for what it is. You may say this is rough talk. Well, it isn't as rough as the actions taken against us. Actions are always spoken louder than words. In our case, we want our words to be more effective than their actions. But they won't be if we soften our language or water down the truth to make it more palatable for everyone for the sake of appeasement.

For those who do care but don't quite understand, you want them to understand our plight. This is why whoever is out front for us must be able to clearly, comprehensively, and boldly explain our condition without capitulating. Explaining is not pleading; it is a science that produces understanding. No matter how clearly you are able to explain things to some people, it won't matter. Even your own people will jump down your throat and challenge you for your views. But they won't challenge someone who has a recorded history of abusing them. This is part of the sickness that is produced by these broken racist systems.

Some black folks will become like defense attorneys for the irrefutable actions of some whites. They are like lap dogs, just chomping at the bit to defend their masters, raising trivial objections and explaining the irrationality of your position. Do you realize how foolish and how sycophantic you look when you do this? If you are going to sign up to represent and be a voice for a people who have no voice, then be bold enough to speak truth to power without bowing down, acquiescing, or genuflecting when it is time to perform.

How can leaders, and pundits alike, want protesters to protest according to a set of guidelines, but won't use their collective voices, power, and influence to do anything about the real problem that keeps producing the derivative problems that stems from this Nation's broken systems? A lot of people have died and are dying. A lot of people have been hurt and are hurting. A lot of people have suffered and are suffering. And they don't know why. They can't figure out why all this is happening. The terms systemic racism, white privilege, and white supremacy have been thrown out there, but no clear explanation as to what these terms actually mean. These terms will be explained in the next chapter.

The objective is to make things less ambiguous. And to give readers clear explanations of the above terms and of other social issues that are plaguing the black and brown communities. It has to be acknowledged that a job was done on black people. Our actions against ourselves and each other says it all. All of the hurt and pain we cause each other has to stop. But it won't stop until we come into a new and higher knowledge and understanding of ourselves, others, and the world at large.

How do we arrive there? It all starts with being more mindful and taking more control of what we mentally consume. If you are what you eat, you should think twice about what you feed your mind. When others are allowed to deposit a body of controlled information in you, you have let a foreign agent in your body and mind that destroys you from the inside out. Look at how we think. Look at how we act. This is not natural. And it is absolutely no accident.

When it is all said and done, we are all the sum total of all of our experiences. Anything that we have ever been through or are going through has a direct and indirect bearing on us. And the greater the ordeal, the greater the effect. There is no denying the fact that we are influenced by everything we see, hear, and go through. I am not making any excuses for unruly, irresponsible, or unlawful behavior for anyone based on what they have been through.   At the same time, if you train someone all their life, which is what you have done with us

TERRY TRIGGS

America, you have groomed and conditioned us. And if you groom and condition a group of people, then you already know how those people will respond under any set of given circumstances. Tell me, is this a lie, or is it the truth?   Armed with this ability to predict future behavior and outcomes, you ingeniously plot ways to capitalize and profit from what you know is coming from conditions you had a hand in creating. You are the hand that rocks the cradle. You have always played the most impactful role in creating the conditions that this country is dealing with. If you take the proliferation of drugs for example, this comes with drug dealers, drug addicts, violence, crack babies, absenteeism fathers because of death and incarceration, and a slew of other tragedies that are spawned from this single weapon of mass destruction called drugs.
 This paves the way for the establishment of the prison industrial complex and mass incarceration. This single escalating series of incidents has other residual effects as well, which, in turn, become the cause of other things. This is just one example of how the influx of drugs in poor communities can morph into other predictable actions that create conditions that serve to bring about the demise of people so afflicted. You are also able to prepare the people for the advent of certain happenings through subtlety to either accept, reject, malign, or defend something or someone.
 This is not a stretch. This happens all the time. But because of your mastery in rocking the cradle, it is almost hard to detect the presence of these subtle psychological influencers. What the eye can't see, what the

ear can't hear, or what the mind can't fathom, it's as if it didn't happen or doesn't exist. The charges being levied here stem from actual events. The upper echelons of government and the wise are well aware of the atrocious acts that have occurred historically and are occurring today that have shaped and continue to shape today's racial climate.

Subtle psychological influences allow the mind to be highly receptive to arguments and positions diametrically opposed to it. How is this accomplished?

This is done by constantly repeating your version of history, events, and conditions. Your aim is to influence thoughts and perceptions. This mass indoctrination and propaganda campaign is intended to overpower the senses through the bombardment of information you provide.

Repetition of something or being able to explain something convincingly is not an accurate measure of the truth of something. Just as not having a huge platform or not being able to explain something convincingly is not an accurate measure that something is untrue. In the next chapter, we will attempt to explain the root of the mindset responsible for much of what is happening in this country and hopefully things will begin to make a little more sense for those still confused and perplexed.

2_ Making Sense of It All

There was an incident at a girl's high school basketball game where Don Imus, a white male commentator, used the one word that is the cardinal sin of all racial epithets when referring to black people. The players kneeled before the game to protest in response to his use of that vulgarity.

Sometime after, maybe a day or so later, a black woman who looked as if she could be around thirty years of age was commenting on the matter to a reporter. After congratulating the girls for their stance, she said that "It makes absolutely no sense why that word would come out of that commentator's mouth the way it did.

I said to myself" as beautiful as you just articulated your point sister, if only you knew who and what you were dealing with, then it would make perfect sense to you why that word flowed so easily not only from his lips but from the lips of many who think and feel exactly like that commentator does. This is more prevalent and deeply rooted than you think. Donald Trump's term as President brought much of that hidden sentiment rushing to the surface exposing the attitudes of many white folks in this country against blacks. So, what I would like to do in this chapter is to attempt to argue a point that brings some form of clarity to those who look at all that is happening as it pertains to race-related issues with the thought in mind, why does this keep happening and for what purpose is it happening? Why is the climate the way it is when it comes to racial issues?

These questions and more need to be answered if we are going to get to the root of this widespread epidemic. The history of racial injustice against blacks in America is long and runs deep and largely stems from an inborn bias and a superiority complex that is fostered through America's institutions. So many people are inherently good that it is difficult for them to fathom how so many have taken up the position of being hateful and insensitive in their language and actions against the black, brown, and other so-called minorities of this nation.

It's one thing when ordinary citizens have negative and hateful attitudes against darker people, but it's even worse when you have those in high-level government positions who have similar attitudes. This not only codifies these attitudes nationally, but these attitudes and their effects cross national borders. Despite the plethora of groups and organizations that have sprung up nationally to counter the injustice that has been practiced unabated in this country for centuries, the animus and vitriol remain. How and why is this happening in this day and time when tolerance is touted from every corner of society?

Yes, the climate of race relations has gradually been getting better throughout the years. Noble reasons for some, and others they could be politically or financially motivated. This still begs the question of why racial injustice still exists. Let us try to make sense of it all so that you will never again be surprised by anyone's words or actions that seem so outside the realm of basic humanity.

After you read this chapter you will stop doubting the reality of what you are witnessing daily. You will stop believing someone's fitting words and believe more in their unjust actions. If a person repeatedly shows you, through their actions, that they do not like you, why would you not believe them? Why would you believe otherwise?

Even if you don't have to be convinced that something is wrong, this still does not make you understand the underlying reasons why or how someone could be so uncaring, unjust, and merciless.

Did you see the complete lack of empathy Derek Chauvin had when onlookers were pleading for him to get off of Mr. George Floyd's neck? Their cries for justice landed on deaf ears. He was completely unmoved by their pleas. What was in him that made him like that? How many times have you seen incidents that were caught on camera that showed the blatant abuse of power and pure unadulterated callousness by white police officers against unarmed blacks? Now imagine what kind of plotting, planning, and scheming goes on behind closed doors with those who think similarly to police officers who are hellbent on administering their own form of justice. When you do this, it will literally shock your conscience to know the depths and lengths to which an entire people's demise is plotted. You can believe this is farfetched if you want to. I just happen to believe otherwise. And discrimination is done so artfully that detection is almost impossible. A highly skilled killer can manufacture a death so masterfully making himself far removed from the cause of death of his victim.

One thing I found that helped me to generally understand other people is by studying and understanding myself. When I look at myself and why I feel the way I feel, why I think the way I think, why I act or behave the way I do, why I believe what I believe, why I have the value system I have, or why I see myself, others and the world the way I do, or why I have the tendencies I have; I found that I was born with certain traits, characteristics, and leanings.

What about you? Have you ever wondered why you have certain tendencies or ways? There are a lot of factors that make any of us the way we are. Through the laws of heredity, we can inherit certain traits genetically. We can be affected by the experiences undergone by our mothers during their pregnancies. Or things could stem from what we learned and from our collective life experiences. It is hard to pinpoint just one single factor. It could be either one of these factors just mentioned, a combination of any of them, or other factors not named. But these are verifiable things that can explain anyone's current mental, moral, or emotional state. This includes both blacks and whites alike.

Let us now put this thing under more of a microscope to examine in detail the specifics of white minds and their natural tendencies. Mind you, I am dealing with generalities that apply to anyone, blacks included. So, when I address whites in this manner, I won't be using a broad brush to paint all whites in a single category. It would be careless, inconsiderate, and irresponsible of me if I did not understand or take into account the many whites who want a better world, or those who strive to be fair, unbiased, and nondiscriminatory. Even if they do nothing or say nothing to bring that better world in, they do not do or say anything to make things worse.

Some people are born into the world with inherent advantages that give them a leg up on others who are not born with those same advantages. If you are born poor and someone else is born rich, do you think there are advantages and disadvantages in either case? What about children who are born and raised in stable home environments where they live in the same home their entire childhood with both parents present? Just suppose this to children who grow up having to relocate many times during their childhood while living in a single-parent household.

Are there advantages and disadvantages in this second scenario? Yes. The long and the short of it is this, some people are born into the world advantaged while others are born disadvantaged. This is irrefutable. Now, what about being born white versus being born black in America? Does being born white in white America come with inherent advantages? Does being born black in white America come with inherent disadvantages? Yes, or no? The answer to both questions is a resounding yes.

Some may argue that it does not matter either way, that everyone is afforded the same opportunities, if this is your position, then you are either delusional, in denial, or just don't know. These facts are beyond dispute. And the only way a fact can be destroyed is if you are presented with a false fact that you accept as true. What is an advantage? It is a better position or condition. It is a benefit or a privilege.

A person who has an advantage over someone else will advance further faster with little to no restrictions, impediments, or roadblocks than those who don't have that same advantage. It's like giving someone a twenty-yard head start in a forty-yard dash. It would be almost impossible to catch someone with that kind of lead with such a short distance to go. So, an advantage from the perspective that we are about to present is a specific privilege that has been bestowed upon someone that enables them to get ahead easily and be the beneficiary of society's perks more effortlessly than others.

White folks are born with this kind of a head start. That's a huge advantage. An undeniable privilege. This privilege is woven into the fabric of every aspect of society. No sane person would say otherwise. If you are famous and you go into a restaurant and because of your fame, your meal is comped, would you reject that free meal? You wouldn't. White people shouldn't be expected to reject something that is conferred upon them because of their whiteness. I doubt any black person would turn something down that was offered for free.

It is no fallacy or accident when we say that we are the last ones hired and the first ones fired. Affirmative action served to give qualified blacks and other so-called minorities a real opportunity for advancement in fields or areas that their blackness or minority status cut them off from. It was a means to try to give a fair shake to those who were systematically excluded solely because of their race, nationality, or gender. Some called this reverse discrimination. But it would not have been necessary if everyone were held and treated as equals in the first place. Since that has never been the case, we have had to fight for every right that we have and take advantage of every opportunity presented.

No one is saying that success is not attainable. There are many successful blacks, some because of affirmative action. Others made it through pure hard work, sacrifice, and determination. No matter how many blacks break through the proverbial glass ceiling, it does not mean the system is not broken, it just means that the few who have made it defied the odds. Some thought that just because Barack Obama became President of the United States black folks finally arrived. But nothing could have been further from the truth. It did show us however the realm of possibility.

Even in that situation, there were a lot of closed-door meetings going on that the general public is not aware of. I'm referring to the consensual selection of Barack Obama as a candidate in the first place. How that process worked is beyond my knowledge. I am not saying this man did not earn his right to be President. But I am saying that politics is a dirty game. It involves lots of wheeling and dealing or quid pro quo. This makes politics a zero-sum game.

We never even consider looking under the surface at some of the motives behind many of the things that happen because of the hoopla that surrounds it. I bet that if you sat down with Barack Obama and you asked him about the grim reality of politics and how those who sit in the seats of power are not inclined to give true justice to black and brown folks if he was so inclined to, he would tell you that no real legitimate effort is made to do the right thing. The moral thing.

Those who sit at the top have always needed the masses on the bottom to support their system. But he will not tell you this because he knows how to play the game. And he has benefitted handsomely by being a good player. He will never expose the inner workings of that diabolical profession.

Through institutional racism, social conditioning, and social engineering, white supremacy is birthed into the psyche of some whites. White supremacy is a sickness. Those who have this mindset think that they have an exclusive right to be atop the world over everyone else. Total world dominance is the goal. Supremacy must be maintained and never relinquished, at all costs no matter the price. Barack Obama becoming President did not sit well with many in the white community. And so when Donald Trump got into office by running on the mantra, "Make America Great Again", this was signaling to all those whites who were incensed that a black man was President of the United States of America that they, whites, are back at the helm. When color consciousness is taught and promoted through education, religion, TV, and Hollywood movies, it is seeding the subconscious mind and conditioning it to see white as the standard by which all other things are measured. When you promote something, in this case, your race, you are advancing or raising your race above all others. This is white supremacy at work.

The aim is to subtly color the perception of others so that they see you as the center or focal point of everything that is right, good, and acceptable. White supremacy is real. There is a class of white folks who cling tightly to the idea that their race is above everyone else's. They promote that ideology around the world. It used to be unsafe for blacks to mention the words white supremacy, not to mention speaking about it in its rawest forms. To this very day, many are bound by fear and their socioeconomic status not to make any waves or cause problems.

People bite their tongues and are not allowed to speak out on controversial or polarizing topics. Topics that make people cringe, feel uncomfortable, or expose dirty truths. They sacrifice this for the sake of acceptance, appeasement, and inclusion. You know the difference between love and hate when it is openly displayed. But what about when it is thinly veiled? Nowadays we are less fooled by the subtle tricks of the wickedly wise. But we are still susceptible to being deceived because we are still not fully convinced that some people, or the government for that matter, is capable of having such racial prejudice or animosity.

Government has the power, the authority, and the resources to immediately fix many of the problems that are plaguing society as a whole and blacks in particular. But they refuse to take the necessary actions or corrective measures to fix society's woes. But why? Let me ask you a question. If I'm a white person, and I'm a racist, and I see my race as being the superior race, and I have inherent biases and prejudices against all other races, and I am tasked with the responsibility of formulating institutions that will make up the world in which me and my people live, do you think that those biases or prejudices will be reflected in those institutions? Think about it. When the educational system was fashioned, when the religious system was established, and when the judicial system was put together, isn't it logical to conclude that those systems will be, at their very core, in favor of whites and against other races?

If I think so little of you, then why would I put you on par with me and my people? I wouldn't. I would keep you subjugated by having interwoven in those systems a means by which our rule is cemented by the implantation and inculcation of our whiteness.

When you think about what produces racism, you have to consider how race consciousness is taught in the extreme and far-reaching way it is. There is nothing wrong with learning about your own culture and heritage. You should be proud of your race. The problem I think becomes when we don't allow room in our minds and hearts for others who are not of our race.

Although the climate is changing that makes speaking on race related issues more acceptable, which is courageous because it is not an easy subject to broach, but I still see that in some cases, qualifying statements are used to soften the blow to let the listener know ""we don't mean it like such and such.", " Even though I am pointing out racism, I am not racist." This is done almost apologetically.

The point I am making is that if racist minds are at the root of the formulation of the aforementioned institutions, this is institutionalized racism. Also known as systemic racism because of how these systems rotate on their own axis and continue through the generations no matter who teaches or operates under those systems.

What makes systemic racism so necessary to uproot is that if left unchecked, it will continue to poison the bloodstream of society and the race issue that everyone is so up in arms about will never go anywhere.

When someone with a racist mind makes laws, what happens? Doesn't that law become a part of the legal system? That system then becomes systemically racist because people operate under that system, and it guides all sorts of decisions and produces all sorts of dire consequences. Evidence of this can be seen in the great disparity that existed in sentencing between possession of crack cocaine and powder cocaine.

This disparity has been well documented and acknowledged as being biased and targeted against black and brown, while lighter sentences were given to whites who had similar amounts of cocaine but a different form of it. This same disparity can be seen in many other laws and mandatory minimum sentences of which we will go more in depth later in this book. So, if a law is changed, that is good, but it does not change what is in a person's mind and heart. The law is only a branch that grew out of a tree that is systemically racist. Cutting off a branch here or there does nothing in the long run.

So, changing laws is a start, but when it is all said and done, the entire tree needs to be uprooted and replaced.

Whether every white person takes advantage of all of the privileges that their whiteness offers them in the ultimate sense is one thing, but that does not mean that as a whole white folks are not privileged in this society. This privilege carries with it an intense sense of entitlement. Believe it or not, there is a certain class of whites who are just as dispensable as the darker peoples of this nation. They are merely casualties of war who have been caught in a net that was not meant for them.

Then you have another class of white folks, as we've previously pointed out, who believe in the idea of white supremacy where no other life has any real value or importance other than their own. When someone thinks like that, it is easy for them to snuff out black lives without conscience. Fear of consequences doesn't even matter either because the system is favored to allow whites to escape justice when their crimes are against a race other than their own. Whites have historically killed blacks and have gotten off scot-free. There are too many historical accounts to mention. In the past when a white person killed a black person, many times an extremely small sentence or even a suspended sentence was given.

Whatever the punishment was, it only amounted to a slap on the wrist. That's even if they were charged in the first place.

Even for some of the most egregious crimes against black men and women, as little as a fine was given. And in some instances that fine was never paid. And no efforts were ever made to collect payment. It really didn't matter because the fine was nominal anyway.

In short, taking the life of a black person by a white person has never been seen as a criminal act. The way white people identify with themselves is different than how they identify with any other race. Black and brown lives have always been expendable and of little value to a certain class of whites. But for whites to put so little value on a life that they had no hand in creating is the epitome of arrogance.

The life of man is the spirit of God in man. When you attempt to kill that spirit by snuffing that life out, you are in fact killing the essence of God in man and your crime of murder extends all the way to the sovereign Lord who created man. This offense is a foul stench in the nostrils of God. This does not move you because you see yourself as a God besides God. Did you know that a crime against God in any capacity has no statute of limitations? You are being tried now and don't even realize it. Your guilt is not even in question. But you are being given respite to repent and reform from your wicked ways.

Man was created in the image and after the likeness of God. And he was given power and dominion to rule God's Creation by His Permission.

Yet, man is missing something on the inside that would enable him to do this. Yes, physically he is alive, but that part of man that makes him really alive isn't until God breathes the breath of life into man. All this means is that the wisdom and knowledge of God must be taught to man. If God does not breathe inspiration into you by whatever means, then you are considered dead, though you are physically alive. If you parallel a man's coming to life with his eventual death, then the same thing that makes him alive, if you take it away, it kills him. Not physically, but mentally, morally, and spiritually. The thing that makes him who he is missing on the inside.

He becomes a living dead thing that needs to be resurrected. His resurrection is tied to how he died. If he is dead because something is missing in his head, then when he receives it, he is able to live. These systems, by their very framework, cuts the underprivileged off from receiving that much needed light or knowledge from God. The intent is to replace God. This can only happen by keeping the people in the dark and ignorant about who they are and who God is. This is what keeps white supremacy alive.

Some whites can't stand the sight of blacks. How is it that you can't stand what you had a hand in producing? When you see blacks acting a fool and doing all kinds of crazy things, you are looking at your own handiwork.

The point is sister, who was so confused as to why that sports commentator could make such racially insensitive remarks towards those black girls, it's because he was speaking from a belief system that reflects his attitude towards blacks. He was speaking from a place of comfortability. Race relations, unless we deal with them head on by going to the root and don't just treat the effects, but the cause that produced the effects, then don't expect to get anything other than what you have been getting.

Those in power will not willingly undo the thing that supports their position in the world.

Don't be confused anymore. People are who they are. But this is a new day and a new time. And that old way of thinking is out of season. A new idea is present that is being resisted against. What is that new idea? Truth and justice are here to replace falsehood and injustice. The former is the way to peace. If peace is what you truly desire, then the choice is simple.

The vast majority of people, from all walks of life, want better. They don't want to be tied to or associated with the dark history of this country's past against blacks. Some will argue that they didn't do any of that. But that does not stop them from benefitting from a society and a system that favors them and disfavors others. It will be hard to undo what has been done. But if any of us wants to live in a better world that many of us desire so much, then we need to do our part in producing that better world. Get into the fight. Stand up. Speak out. Get into positions where change can happen. Then have the courage and fortitude to make those changes. And in time, perhaps, things will get better.

3_ Much More than Police Brutality

It has taken quite some time, but because of the killing of George Floyd in Minneapolis, Minnesota on May 25, 2020, mass protests have forced the hand of many in the field of politics, business, and even the world of sports to take a stand on social justice issues. Although many have taken a stand, they have been motivated to do so for many different reasons. Some for political reasons, some for financial reasons, and others because they are guided by their conscience.

The climate in the country is making it so that you won't be standing on an island by yourself for voicing your opposition to the way things are, not only in policing but as it relates to other social justice issues as well. This has not always been the case. Since things have reached a boiling point with this nationwide and global outcry against police brutality, things have been fast-tracked by government officials to take some form of remedial action. At the forefront of the changes being advocated for is defunding the police to allocate that funding elsewhere.

This has caused a backlash, uproar, and resistance arguing that people want the police to be completely dismantled. This has proven not to be the case at all. The messaging is often politicized and purposefully misconstrued and given a narrative that fits an agenda that keeps the new era of Jim Crow intact. These knee-jerk responses are there to protect an institution that in practice, seems to do everything except protect and serve the communities they are supposed to protect and serve.

This is evidenced in how often black and brown folks are consistently preyed upon, terrorized, and in many instances, killed unjustifiably by police officers. This malfeasance is not limited to some police officers alone. This extends to and includes those who are judges, prosecutors, politicians, and even those in the medical, business, and scientific fields. They hide their misconduct under the color of law, medicine, and science to give their racial biases a semblance of legality, nobility, and credibility which legitimizes their actions.

Just two short months before George Floyd's murder, Breonna Taylor was gunned down in Louisville, Kentucky by officers from their drug unit after a "no-knock warrant". Come to find out, the suspect they were looking for was already in police custody.

Her boyfriend, a legal gun owner, not knowing who barged their way into her apartment, shot an officer in his leg. He was charged and the charges were later dropped. Sadly though, Breonna Taylor was killed in the process. She is another casualty in a long list of killings of blacks by police officers.

Nothing substantial has changed since Breonna Taylor's and George Floyd's death. There have been multiple deadly encounters by the police since then. One of the more horrific instances involved a 13-year-old named Adam Toledo in Chicago, on April 14, 2021. And even though he was accused of being in possession of a firearm, when he followed the orders of the officer to put his hands up, he complied and was still shot dead. Compliance is no guarantee that you won't end up dead after an encounter with the police.

Officers are trained professionals who should be able to discern between threats and non-threats. Sometimes that line might be thin, but this is where their training should kick in. A twenty-year-old black man named Daunte Wright who was shot dead by police a couple of days earlier on April 11, 2021. Hanging air fresheners supposedly triggered the traffic stop. Police say it was because of having an expired registration. Whatever motivated the stop, things ended when a 26-year police veteran said she mistook her gun for a taser and shot Daunte. No offense he committed should have risen to a death sentence.

April 21, 2021, Andrew Brown Jr. was shot dead by multiple police during an attempt to serve a search warrant. Even being shot in the back of the head. What message is this sending to the rest of us? "That no matter how much you whoop and holler about what we are doing, we will still kill you. Your life, your black life, means nothing to us." Two years after a police cover-up of Ronald Greene's death on May 10, 2019, a bodycam video was released that showed an entirely different story. The brutal, callous, and indifferent way those state troopers handled Ronald Greene is another example of why police reform is needed. He complied and showed no resistance, yet he died.

So, what can you do to comply, comply and you still die? It's a no-win situation. This points to something more than bad policing. I'm afraid that no matter what reforms are made, the problem with police brutality will only persist. Black voices who are on the opposite side of the fence on the race issue or who have opposing views are strategically hand-picked to put a black face on issues that reflect the views of those who defend the actions of police who kill unarmed black men and women. The story never deals with the issue at hand. It always veers toward defending the police who unjustifiably kill in the line of duty.

I won't discount the rigors, hardships, and inherent dangers in being a police officer. But when you are wrong, like any of us, you should be held accountable. No one should be above the law. Yet you operate with impunity as if you are. How can you ever expect to make any headway when the problem of what is happening is not acknowledged? How can a consensus be reached when what needs to be done about policing is seen so differently by different people?

There is no doubt in my mind that race plays a major role in what is transpiring with these deadly encounters by the police against blacks. Others say it has nothing to do with race. I will say that unless the problem is honestly addressed, you can continue to expect more of the same, and even worse. What compounds the problem is when you have ideological hardliners who are hellbent on being a stumbling block to progress. These ideologies are unyielding in their opposition to the people's cry for the right to be fairly heard.

With so many smart people in leadership, it used to baffle me why they failed to hit the nail on the head on such an obvious problem as police brutality, excessive force, and unjustifiable killings. That is until I reflected more on the cyclical nature of history and how the atrocities of the past still exist today. Things are just packaged differently. Many of us never notice the hidden forces at work manipulating events and circumstances that determine certain outcomes. The more advanced society gets, the face of racism uncannily contorts itself to fit the changing times.

There are a couple of Black Fox News contributors who are, in my opinion, lackeys and sycophants. They are foolhardily in love with the tormentors of black folks. They are kalsomined and suffer from the Stockholm syndrome.

You may say that I should not resort to this kind of talk, but I have a right to my opinion of them as they do when they speak on race-related issues. Besides, I don't have a bit in my mouth that prevents me from calling out token blacks who perform for their masters. There have always been, in every generation, Uncle Tom. This generation is no different.

The protests following the killing of Daunte Wright was highly criticized for crossing the line of what they consider to be peaceably assembling to protest. This goes back to what we said in Chapter One about the types and styles of protests. Some media commentators continued to change the narrative evading the real underlying issue. That issue is that another innocent black man was unjustifiably killed at the hands of white police. This is the same old song and dance. When is it going to be time for a different tune? I'll tell you; when we come together in a broader sense with more concrete planned action to confront the evil of white supremacy.

Would these encounters have the same tragic end if the person was white instead of black? How many deaths, and you have to excuse me because I am not working with any statistics, but comparatively speaking, how many white people die at the hands of the police under similar circumstances? I would like to know the answer to that question. No matter how you slice this pie, race is part of the filling. And for the record, I do believe that you have good police officers who sincerely want to protect and serve. I'm not sure I agree with the percentages being given about how many so-called bad apple cops are giving good police a bad name in comparison to the good ones.

But what I do believe and what I will say is that these problems are systemic. A major theme that is central to the concept of this book deals with systemic racism, so we will revisit this term often. As long as the system stays the same, that system will continue to churn out what we are seeing. When someone is remote from the effects of bad policing, it does not resonate the same as someone who is directly impacted. So, the need for change is not taken as seriously. This is why the pace is so slow to enact changes that can curb these incidents of police brutality against black people.

Again, what if whites were the victims of being killed by black police officers at the same rate and for the same reasons as white officers killing blacks? What kind of response do you think you would get? How many charges would be filed? And how many convictions would those charges produce? I want you to think about that. Do you know how quickly things would change if the above were the case?

Things would literally change overnight. If the rooster ever came home to roost, that would be a different story. As long as blacks continue to be the victims in these encounters, oh well. God forbid these horrible tragedies enter into white homes. That closeness will make you respond quickly and effectively. But when you are unable to identify with the oppressed because you don't know what oppression and injustice feels like, then you can afford to dilly-dally around.

There is no doubt that police brutality needs to be addressed. At the same time, I would like to make the point of saying that in addition to police brutality, there are more less visible forms of brutal treatment against blacks that have a similar damaging effect. We will be pointing this out in the many institutions that are not as open to public scrutiny because the damage is on the mental, moral, and spiritual level. This microscopic activity cannot be seen with the naked eye and therefore is unable to be highlighted the same way policing is. If it wasn't for so many recorded incidents of excessive force and deadly encounters by police, would we be at the point we are now of having so much attention and focus on police brutality and police reform?

How many police reports would accurately reflect what actually happened when a black life is unjustly taken? How much coverup would there be? You already see false reports being written even when video evidence shows a contrary account of events. If these recordings didn't exist how much would be known? Or would things be swept under the rug as they have always been? That is gall. And it speaks to the comfortability of being protected by the blue wall of silence and corruption within some police departments.

The overall lack of transparency points to something not being right. Wouldn't you want to be transparent and open if you knew you did everything right and had nothing to hide? But that wall is showing signs of cracking. And it is only a matter of time before it comes crashing down. Police training can and will help in many cases. Retraining police is not the end all solution because no amount of training will erase an officer's belief system if it is rooted in racism. Or an attitude rooted in white supremacy.

Some officers will still push the envelope because they won't be able to shake their deeply held beliefs. It's like expecting a drug addict to shake their dependency on drugs without any support. When you have a penchant for something, it will cause you to act on what it is you seem to like doing irrespective of the consequences. Obviously, I'm not a law enforcement professional, however, I think part of the training should include proper threat assessment. By this, I mean that police should use their training and apply that training according to situational factors to determine the existence of a threat.

If a threat is deemed present, what level or degree of threat is it?

Based upon the level or degree of threat the officer is faced with or is tasked with handling, there should be an appropriate approach to that perceived threat. Once those factors no longer exist, then deescalate, or rollback the amount of force being applied in accordance with and proportionate to the decrease in the threat. Training should entail factoring in intangibles like mental health issues that require special handling. A mentally handicapped person poses the greatest threat to themselves. Most of the time an officer may not be armed with the knowledge of a person's mental health history. So, training that enables an officer to detect if someone is under the influence is a type of training that can detect certain mental handicaps. I know that situations are fluid and require their response. In the event training like this is possible, then it should be considered. If it is in place already, then it needs to be practiced more.

Policing is different in black or predominantly black neighborhoods as opposed to white or predominantly white neighborhoods. This goes back to the identity factor that will be explained in upcoming chapters. Police presence is different. One argument is that more police are needed in the black community because the crime rate is higher there. Let's just say this for the record, all black people are not criminals or engaged in criminal activity. But there is this preconceived notion that we all are, so we are all put in the same category. This stereotyping places all black people who encounter an officer who thinks like this at a disadvantage from Jump Street.

What you do not hear a lot about is the causes of the commission of most of the crimes committed by blacks or in black communities. In Chapter Seven on Criminal Justice Reform, we will introduce a term that Dr. Martin Luther King Jr. used in one of his speeches. That term is 'derivative crimes'. This will point to who the real criminals are. No one is born a criminal or predisposed to commit a crime. However, environmental factors can create a very high likelihood of a person engaging in criminal activity. Remove those factors, and crime reduction will happen. When the need to do something is removed, then there is no need to do it.

However, the powers that be are well aware of this. If you can study fires and their causes and how best to prevent them, then you can use this same scientific approach to study crime, its causes, and how best to prevent it? But why would you do that when crime is big business for you? As this chapter suggests in its title, the issue of police brutality is a pressing matter that needs to be dealt with, but I want to propose that there are other things that are just as dangerous and deadly, in effect, that transpire that don't get the attention that police misconduct does. That's because there is no cellphone video to capture what is invisible on the surface. How can you notice something if it is hiding in plain sight? You can't.

Ever since slavery blacks have had to deal with racial injustice and discrimination on massive levels. Laws, both written and unwritten, were instituted that sought to keep blacks from equal access to things such as good housing, adequate healthcare, quality education, loans at affordable rates, and so on. All of this is well known. Back then, during the era known as Jim Crow, there was no mistaking what was going on or who the enemy was. We did not have to guess or wonder. The things that were done to us were not done in a sneaky way.

No attempts were made to disguise this period of diabolical wicked and unjust treatment. Things were blatant. Not nowadays. Where has Jim Crow gone? Has it simply vanished? Is it a relic of the past? What has changed from then until now? Not much at all. We are still discriminated against. We are still disproportionately affected in the above-mentioned areas. The only difference between then and now is the level of sophistication involved in the application of these prejudices.

Things today are more subtle and indirect. Instead of white hooded robes as their calling card, now they wear black robes, police uniforms, and a suit and tie. But the idea is still the same. To subdue and subjugate; to deny and deprive; and to torture and torment. So, where's Jimmy? Jimmy has never gone anywhere. This new Jim Crow era that we are living in is only a new version of the same old thing. Unless you are a student of history or are conscious of the various social elements that affect our condition, then you will think everything is just fine. That things were never better.

I'm here to tell you that nothing could be further from the truth. We are still treated like second class citizens. I'm speaking for the whole of us and not the few who have risen above their condition of poverty. Since things are not as open as what we see with police brutality, we need to also focus on other areas and their impact on race relations. Education has a function and a purpose. Religion has a function and a purpose. Government has a function and a purpose. If none of these systems are producing the results they are supposed to produce, then this should make us pause for cause.

What I want to get across and what we will uncover is that it is deeper and more problematic than police brutality alone. Policing is one arm of a larger body. A body that is full of systems that have white supremacist elements coursing through its veins. The entire educational system needs to be uprooted. The entire religious system needs to be uprooted. The political system as a whole, needs to be uprooted. The entire economic system needs to be uprooted. And the entire criminal justice system needs to be uprooted. I don't want us to lose sight of a much bigger problem that none of us are exempt from.

At the same time, I don't want to give the impression that I'm glossing over the painful deaths that many families have suffered from and irreparable damage from rogue cops or vigilantes. That madness has to end. And it will end. Either by their own volition or by forces arrayed to do what they won't do on their own. All I'm getting at is that we cannot afford to lose this present moments momentum to tackle one issue when many more can be added to the slate. I want to show you how a commonplace practice that is small on the surface, but when you look deep enough into it, it will reveal just how intricate and how pervasive systemic racism operates economically that contributes to the huge wealth gap between blacks and whites.

The economic system is as poisoned as all the other systems are.

Its purpose and design are to keep the rich, rich and the poor, poor. There is a practice that we've come to accept as a natural way of doing business, so it doesn't immediately raise any red flags. Debt is the secret of how banking institutions and credit card companies siphon money in an endless stream from the already anorexic pockets of the poor right into the overstuffed pockets of the filthy rich.

Debt, of any kind, unless it is used to invest in a Bonafede financial venture to make money, is a tool to keep those who already don't have money from rising out of poverty. When you are already poor you are unable to afford to pay cash for a lot of things. What does this then lead to?

This forces you to secure loans with excessively high interest rates, that's even if you can qualify to get a loan. If you do qualify, your mortgage rate or payment plan to pay for a home, a car, furniture, or credit card debt, especially if you don't have good credit, you will end up paying substantially more for the same thing as someone who can afford to pay cash. Let's say you want to purchase a home for $100,000.00. How much do you think a person who can afford to pay cash or make a larger down payment will pay for that home as opposed to a poor person? If an all cash offering was made on the home, after all other associated costs, you will pay pretty close to what the asking price is.

If you are poor you need to secure a loan to buy the home, and don't have poor credit on top of that. Because the small incremental increase of a percentage point or two on your interest rate could cost you tens of thousands of dollars more over a thirty-year mortgage. And when it is all said and done, you may end up paying $225,000.00 to $250,000.00 for the same $100,000.00 home. You will pay more in interest than what the principal cost of the home is.
Home ownership for that person is virtually impossible. So they are forced to rent.

Renting is a vehicle that keeps many people from the path of financial freedom and wealth building. After fifteen years of home ownership and fifteen years of renting, you are ahead owning your own home even if your mortgage payments, in the beginning were higher than what you would have paid in rent. After only a few short years your rent would have increased annually while your fixed mortgage rate remains the same throughout the duration of the mortgage. No to mention your accrued equity. The above is only one of many examples to choose from that could be used to show how the economic system is tilted favorably towards the rich and is setup to force the poor to use infinitely more expensive alternatives to obtain the same home, car, or other property.

This keeps the poor in debt and in financial straits and to live from paycheck to paycheck servicing debts that will take a lifetime to pay.

When black people die, instead of passing on wealth to our children, we pass on debt. This doesn't include the threat of losing everything while we are living, being heavily fined, or having our interest rates raised because of a missed or late payment. Since we know who is more likely to miss or be late on a payment, we know who will be predominantly penalized. The economic system is as much a part of the entire infrastructure of white supremacy as all of the other systems are. Blacks, Latinos, and poor Whites have always been the fodder to feed this system. And there are others who unknowingly furthers the aims and objectives of the elites who are very detailed oriented in how they put the economic system and other systems together. If something was not factored in at an earlier stage of a particular system's development because it was missed or not yet in existence, it is quickly added or incorporated in such a way to steer the effects towards their original aim of keeping blacks marginalized.

In order to facilitate this feat, each system has subsystems that provides logistical support in the form of seemingly innocuous services that give the appearance of being right or normal, but they always end in financial ruin that is hard, if not outright impossible to recover from.

These are the invisible forces that we have always been up against which has made their presence and the threat they pose undetectable and rendered us incapable of being truly financially independent or taking the necessary steps to make the best financial decisions for ourselves. Take a lending officer at a bank for example. This lending officer operates under a system he or she did not create. A system that was already in place when he or she started working there. Yet this person facilitates a system of economic oppression. This system sucks the lifeblood out of the poor because of prewritten policies that puts blacks at a disadvantage. So when a worker acts in that capacity they operate from a set of pre-established guidelines. These guidelines ensure the perpetuity and effectiveness of predatory lending practices that targets the poor.

How many of us have taken the time to consider the possibility that these practices may be socially or racially motivated and intended to strategically deprive the poor of their already thinly stretched resources? This practice is done on an international scale as well involving poor resource rich continents like Africa. When it comes to economic growth and prosperity, no matter how harmless something appears when it comes to any institution erected by this world, they are all designed to squeeze the lifeblood out of us and keep us from rising mentally, morally, spiritually, and economically. The "us" is not limited to black people.

I would like to offer a hypothesis in regards to the infamously coined term, 'the talented tenth' widely attributed to W.E.B. Du Bois. He adopted it from a white man named Henry Lyman Morehouse, which is where Morehouse College takes its name from. When you trace the roots of who, why, and what gave rise to this term, it raises the very real possibility that this concept, for similar reasons, could very easily be transferred over from education to the arena of economics to accomplish the same purpose. Mr. Morehouse said the following; "In the discussion concerning Negro education we should not forget the talented tenth man. An ordinary education may answer for the nine men of mediocrity; but if this is all we offer the talented tenth man, we make a prodigious mistake." Why? Because, Morehouse continues, "the tenth man, with superior natural endowments, symmetrically trained and highly developed, may become a mightier influence, a greater inspiration to others than all the other nine, or nine times nine like them.". This is quoted from 100 Amazing Facts About the Negro by Henry Louis Gates Jr. If ten percent of blacks could be given a more liberal education than the other ninety percent to provide a particular balance and provide a particular function, then it could provide the same balance and function along with the added bonus of having the visual optics to give the illusion of a greater success of a people whose greater percentage, much greater percentage, are living below the poverty line.

When talking about the economic plight of black people it is hard to do so without going back in history to perhaps the single greatest economic destructive act in our history in America. A fabricated incident that a black man had 'assaulted' a white woman in an elevator led to the most violent massacre of blacks by whites in U.S. history. This caused the most economically advanced blacks in America to lose all they had built. I'm referring to what is historically known as Black Wall Street in Tulsa, Oklahoma in 1921, in the Greenwood District.

An estimated three hundred, some say more, black people were killed. And guess what? Not a single white person was ever arrested or charged. But up to 6,000 thousand black people were arrested. And after the eighteen-hour attack, the Greenwood District was destroyed beyond repair. This history has been buried for decades. The hand that rocks the cradle is always many layers removed from the scene of the crime. There are no eyewitnesses. No physical evidence. Only circumstantial evidence. Which is never enough to convict.

We can't remain ignorant if we are going to effectively deal with what is going on. We must become learned enough to be able to defend our most basic rights. To do this we need the unity necessary to make our fight for justice and equality on all fronts yield results. Lastly, as this chapter signals, police brutality is a real problem that is in need of real solutions. And unfortunately, like we've pointed out, if it wasn't for the video exposure of these acts, they would not be the center of focus as they have become.

Police brutality is only the tip of the iceberg. The bulk of the problem isn't noticeable unless and until we penetrate beneath the surface. Overall, police need to be more transparent. Held more accountable. Undergo extensive retraining. And the protective shield of immunity needs to be removed.

4_ Educational and Religious Caveats

Education is important. Religion is too. But for the purposes of this book, I want to put forth a couple of warnings about the quality of education and the type of religion that are contributing factors to the race issue. It is a type of warning that exhorts someone away from certain acts, practices, or involvements. It is an explanation to prevent misinterpretation. It is a cautionary measure to be strongly considered when evaluating, interpreting, or doing something.

A caveat emptor is a principle in commerce that without a warranty, the buyer assumes all the risks. This is where the phrase, let the buyer beware comes from. Without verifiable assurances, then you should beware of accepting anything on face value. One of the main avenues that feeds the minds of all Americans from an early age is the educational system. Through education many of the subtle psychological influencers earlier spoken of are implanted. Proper education seeks to unleash the inner potential in each person by cultivating and bringing out the innate gifts, skills, and talents that each person has been blessed with. Proper education does not inculcate. It is not simply rote learning.

Good teaching encourages you to become a critical thinker. A producer. Teaching is a gift that carries with it certain intangibles that can't in and of itself be taught. You can learn the particulars, but the other stuff you have to have a knack for. A love for. The educational system, the version of education that many of us have been given, is such that it should not be taken on face value. Because on face value, education is something that we all should strive to advance in.

In truth, education, proper education, is good and necessary to bring out of you what the Creator has deposited within you. There is an entire world wrapped up in you that needs to be unwrapped in order for the gifts you were blessed with to manifest. The structure of the education system is tiered. The most privileged in society are on the top tier and are given the best quality education. This education positions them to maintain their elite status that allows their stranglehold on the world stage to continue.

In this chapter we want to point out that any institution that has not produced what it was supposedly designed to produce, then be warned. When what you get is not what has been touted, then something is definitely amiss. Look into the educational system to see if it is in any way attributable for the condition of the people who have been educated in that system. I want to say right off that the charge that is being levied here is that the educational system has played a very significant role in fostering and fashioning the minds of those who would later become what is considered the dregs of society. The so-called miscreants.

From the earliest stages of a person's development, the educational system has been one of the most pivotal tools in training and conditioning people to fit into an already set of existing and established systems. Those being religious, political, judicial, economical, and social. This chapter is perhaps the crux of what this little book is about. Because if the hand that rocks the cradle rules the world, then the educational system is the main institution that does the rocking. Who is more responsible, the potter or the clay? Who shapes who?

If you shape the minds of the people through various mediums, then what you get is what you get. What you see in the streets of America is a product of your making. Isn't this what you wanted? A dumb, docile, and foolish people that you could easily control, rule, and profit from? I didn't say that people are not responsible for their own behavior and actions, but who is more responsible? Aren't you the potter? You can't cast blame on us for reflecting what you made us into.

The principle is well established that if you train up a child in the way that child shall go, when that child gets older it will not depart from that training. I won't go into the vast differences between training and teaching except to say that very little teaching goes on in the public educational school system. As this writer has pointed out in other writings, there are different classes who are afforded different types and qualities of education. In short, the schooling that the elites receive is leaps and bounds above what the poor receive.

I would like to present a quote on education by former President Woodrow Wilson. He said, "We want a class of persons to have a liberal education and we want another class of persons, a very much larger class, of necessity, to forego the privilege of a liberal education and fit themselves to perform specific difficult manual tasks.". The structure and real purpose of this present educational system is based upon the elites being supported by the masses on the bottom, the working class. It is not in the best interest of white supremacy to ensure that every American receives a quality education.

The above bears witness that there are classes of education. The one given to the elite or privileged. And the others given to the masses or underprivileged. This latter is so inferior that it weakens instead of strengthens. Trains instead of teachers. It makes you fit into an already existing system instead of forging a way for yourself. Your desire to create something for yourself is killed. Built-in invisible parameters are placed around your mind on what you can or cannot be or achieve.

Children are told that they should stay in school. I agree that schooling and getting a good education is necessary. At the same time, we have to acknowledge that the educational system as it is needs reforming. Even if you take race out of the equation. The statistics of where America ranks among other industrialized nations in science and math is abysmal.

This does not include the millions of Americans who are functionally illiterate. Look at the dropout rate. Of those who do graduate high school, how many go on to college?   Now compare these statistics between blacks and whites and the numbers are even more staggering.

Just as Woodrow Wilson promulgated, that a larger class of persons should forego a liberal education so that they never aspire beyond being assigned specific difficult manual tasks. What is the subliminal message here? The subliminal message is that it is okay to use your hands but not your mind. Your body, but not your brain. Leave the tasks that require a more cerebral approach to us while you stay where you have been trained to fit in.

I would like to quote, once again, from a man who I think is greatly misunderstood, but the power of his mind and the profound wisdom he possesses is undeniable, the Most Honorable Elijah Muhammad. He said that "Knowledge is the result of learning and is a force or energy that makes its bearer accomplish or overcome obstacles, barriers, and resistance.". Knowledge is the antidote and is one of the most essential needs that all human beings need to empower themselves. The only way an obstacle, a barrier, or anything resists you, is because you don't have the requisite knowledge.

If you and I have been educated, what have we learned that will allow us to overcome the many obstacles that are in life's path? How much do we learn about life, the world, or ourselves in school? You may say that it is the parents' responsibility to teach their children these things. But guess what, the parents were trained by you too, so where are they going to learn it from?

Look at the many obstacles and barriers that we are faced with but do not have the necessary knowledge to effectively overcome them. Instead, life experiences become the teacher that we rely on to teach us. Sometimes this means learning things the hard way and at a much greater cost. Proponents of education may not look favorably upon this critique. Like I said, and it bears repeating, education, proper education, is a vital necessity and highly beneficial for the advancement of an individual, a people, and a nation.

But when a large chunk of people are fed an inferior quality education, then it will not only be reflected in their own lives, but society as a whole will suffer as a result too. So the price you pay in depriving people of a quality education will not only hurt them, but you too. In the end, this will be the undoing of what you have built because what you built was for purposes other than right. No matter how educated or successful a black person becomes, they will never be able to rise above the condition of the many blacks who are like all of the other crabs still stuck in the barrel.

You are only a crab who has been let out of the barrel and showcased to the world or other blacks to say see, we have come a long way. And we have, but just not far enough. You want the message to be that this is a fair society where everyone is afforded equal opportunities. That's a lie. The same opportunities exist, but everyone does not have equal access to them. Don't be fooled, be warned. This is the caveat.

What do you think the glass ceiling is all about? It is an imaginary level to which we were never taught or expected to go beyond. Many blacks have not only broken that ceiling, but they have shattered the ceiling that was intended to place a plateau on how far any of us could ascend in this world. You may wonder why is there so much talk about race. This kind of talk is in response to those who made it about race.

Blacks didn't invent the race card. Blacks didn't invent this racial divide. The white power structure is the culprit here. What you see is the effect of a cause that you initiated a long time ago that has not went anywhere.

If you are what you eat, then when you consume an education that is poisoned by racism, then your condition will be reflective of what you have ingested. A poison is any substance that is taken into the body that can, through its chemical reaction, cause injury, impairment, and even death. Racism is a poison. And when it is introduced into the mind through education, it too can cause injury, impairment, and even death. Not a physical death, but the death of the mental powers, hopes, and aspirations of the individual so affected.

Having an inferior education has many negative side effects. One of the things at the top of the list is poverty. Lack of having a proper education, as we have said, limits employment opportunities. It also impedes creative thinking. Poverty is a dangerous weapon used to keep poor people deprived, dependent, and despondent. Poverty becomes the cause of a bevy of predicted behavior patterns and actions that are preventable. If this is the case then why hasn't any corrective action taken place?

The time is out from listening to sweet-sounding words and false promises that are not followed up with proper action. No one who is in a position of power that can produce real change is really concerned about making changes that can instantly and drastically improve the lives of millions of people. When things are consistently spoken about and acknowledged and still nothing happens, this suggests either hollow words on behalf of those who admit the existence of systemic racism in education, or an even more powerful element that is resistant and not as inclined to remove their oppressive hand from the necks of blacks who are poverty stricken or anyone else who is disenfranchised in any way.

The Honorable Marcus Garvey stated the following, "The present day negro or colored intellectual is no less a liar and a cunning thief than his illustrious teacher. His occidental(western) collegiate training only fits him to be a rogue and a vagabond, and a seeker after the easiest and best by following the line of least resistance. He's lazy, dull, and uncreative. His purpose is to deceive the less fortunate of his race, and, by his wiles ride easily into position and wealth at their expense, and thereafter agitate for and seek social equality with the creative and industrious whites. To every rule, however, there is the exception, and in this case, it must be applied.".

Marcus Garvey gave a scathing rebuke of a certain class of educated blacks who are patsies who do the bidding of the intellectual class of whites. Unfortunately, there are blacks who prey upon their own people's misery, disadvantaged position, and station in life. This type of betrayal by some black leaders makes it hard for anyone who is honest, sincere, and able to help from garnering the broad support needed. Too many of those who came before the one or ones who are the real deal were fraudsters.

They mortgaged the plight of their people for mere pence's from those in power. This is why Jesus' job was so hard because all that came before him were liars, thieves, and robbers. The people were deceived, lied to and taken advantage of. All in the name of God or a good cause. It is wise to be cautious, apprehensive, and even suspicious of those who come in the same path no matter what they profess.

It was Jesus' intense love for those his life was sacrificed for that enabled him to be falsely accused. All the while hoping that as long as the people for which he came eventually recognized him by his works and not just his words. Jesus represented a truth that if we knew it, it would make us free. What do you think that truth is? Could it be the truth of ourselves, others, and our condition? Could it be the truth of the reality of God, the devil, and the time in which we live?

The Art of War says, which was elaborated on in The Master's Deck, that those who "...know themselves and not their enemy, are assured of victory only half the time. And those who know their enemy, but not themselves, were also assured of victory half the time. But those who know both themselves and their enemy are assured of victory every time.". When anyone stands before you, whether they be black or white, always search out their motive. Look behind their words. One way is to check their track record of service. Look at their résumé. Suspicion is not always good, but because very few are selfless enough to serve your best interest, you have to make sure that those who are out front are not pretenders. You and I have to choose who we put our support behind. That choice should never be decided for us by those who have never been for us. When the white power structure backs a black person you should be very wary.

If history is our guide, then our most faithful and effective leaders have always been vilified by the opposition. Usually when a black leader is really for his or her people, the government won't sanction that person, and that person is never spoken of well by government officials or through major news outlets which are ran by the elite. I want to touch on religion from the perspective of how race has played a major factor in our sick love for those who oppress us. Worship of God is one thing. But when God is whitewashed to foster in religious adherents a psychological dependence on everything white, then a person's love and worship of God has been supplanted by love and worship of white people.

Religion has sanctified an attitude of white being better based upon a belief that black people were destined to be the servants of white people. This has been depicted and misinterpreted in the story of Ham, one of the sons of Noah. Organized religion has moved far from its original purpose of reuniting and reconnecting the soul of man with his Creator, into being a chief tool of control. What is more powerful than affecting an entire people than infecting entire religions with a theology of white supremacy? The bloodstream of religion, and it pains me to say this, but it has coursing through its veins an ideology that is infused with racism.

And guess who the central figure in all of this is? Jesus. The man that so many black people are in love with, and rightfully so. If you are honest and don't deal in emotionalism, the brand of Christianity that has been forced upon us was tainted and meant to make us fall in love with white people by having us fall in love with their version of Jesus. Jesus is not the problem here. The problem lies with those who have painted him in a different light to serve their wicked and diverse ends.

So, what you have arising out of these two systemically racist institutions are two complexes that are self-destructive to both races. You have at the end of this training ground, education; and false worshipping tool, religion; the emergence of a white superiority complex and a black inferiority complex. The former produces and attitude of being better and more worthy. The latter produces feelings of inadequacy and low self-esteem. Where there is either extreme reticence or extreme aggression. There is a psychology to why people think the way they do, and these two complexes are a big part of that.

Out of all the billions of people on the planet, how many would you say belong to some form of religion? I would say a very large amount. Why then does it appear as if religion has had no real transformative power in people's lives? For this very reason, people have discarded religion as it is in its present form and have inclined more to spiritual principles that have nothing to do with religion.

Did you know that if you submit to something, no matter what it is, then you become that which you submit to? If, according to the language of the Bible, Satan deceived the whole world, then does that deception extend to and include religion? And if so, what aspects of religion have we been deceived about? You have to think about these things because our belief system may be rooted in a false representation of God, devil, and Jesus.

Do you even think this is remotely possible? Do you think that we should seriously reconsider what we have been taught religiously by those who at one point in time locked us out of the Bible. By locked out I mean that the Bible was kept from us. And finally, these same people gave us their interpretation and explanation of the scriptures. An interpretation and explanation that put them in the most favorable light possible, and us in the worst.

If I know who God is, who devil is, who Jesus is, and I can make all of them other than who they really are, then that is a masterstroke in not only control but in how you believe.   First you teach us against ourselves forming certain attitudes. Then you follow that up with a belief system rooted in a lie.

When you can take God from a material being and make Him immaterial and make Him totally inconsistent with the human being, then you have stripped that people from their connection to God in a realistic way. They want us to believe that the only way we could ever meet God is in the sky when we die. This is pie in the sky teaching that many of our people are starting to reject.

Then you scare us into this belief by hanging over our heads a fictitious devil who you say we will meet, again, when we die, if we don't profess out belief how and in who you say we should. The picture of hell is painted as this fiery place where there is an intense perpetual searing pain.

I agree with that description but I've also come to believe that I can experience that while I'm living and don't have to wait until I die. Hell is what many black people have and continue to experience under your rule. Our lives have been a living hell. And finally, to put the icing on the cake, you took a good man, Jesus, and painted him white. Why did you do that? What was your purpose? What did you hope to accomplish by making the most believed figure in the scriptures and make him white when there is, from the very same Bible, plenty of evidence that says otherwise?

By doing this, do you think that this is a contributing factor, whether large or small, that plays a part in the race dilemma of today? I would say that it does. For believers in God, there is no Being more powerful than God. It makes no difference what name you call on God by. My question is this, if God is this powerful Being, and He is, and yet many of us who have submitted to Him are weak, then we must ask ourselves have we been submitting to God in truth or a version of God that has been given to us?

The manifestation of the fruit of our submission will be revealed in our lives in some way that is not abstract. If you don't know the truth of God, devil, or Jesus, then you are only able to engage in ritualistic practices and never get to the principles contained in religion that harmonizes with human nature. This is why I said that organized religion, in the form that it has been given to us, has been used as a chief controlling tool. People are deprived of power when you make the power of God remote from the individual.

Nothing is more personal to black folks or evokes more emotion than religion, so don't think that I am attacking anyone's belief system. I'm not. I'm challenging us to look at every institution that has been given to us with a critical eye. The institution of religion is a part of these institutions that singularly may not do the job of ensnaring us, but as a collective and in conjunction with the others, it plays an important role in race relations. This is a part of the treatise on race relations. We have to take a look at everything. And as special and as personal as our relationship is with God, we are justified in making sure we have it right to the best of our ability. Fortunately for us we have some very conscious black preachers whose theological teachings have veered away from the slave preaching of times past. So, take these educational and religious warnings to heart and as a means to become more aware of what you consume because it affects your mental, moral, and spiritual state of being.

5_ Those who Govern and the Governed

When you are the head of a household, then everyone in that household is under your care, supervision, and guidance. And everyone in that household is bound by the rules of your authority. When those who have been living under you go out into the world, they will reflect everything they have learned living under your authority. How you govern your house can be seen in what you produce. Your family's actions will be seen as a reflection of your type and style of leadership in your household.

Some laws in some states hold a parent responsible for the actions of their children. After all, your children are your responsibility, and up to a certain point you can be held accountable for their actions. So, if they damage property for example, then you, as the parent will bear the responsibility of having to foot the bill to fix or replace what was destroyed by your children. This is an understandable and acceptable practice. Why should someone else have to pay for something they didn't do? Or why should someone not have to pay for something their child has done?

No one should have to bear another's burden, but when it comes to parental responsibility, that's a different story.

Now once your children are grown and go out on their own, then you as a parent are free from certain things when it involves your children.

Your children, no matter how old they get, or how far they move on from you, will always carry with them what has been instilled in them by you. That imprint will be with them for the rest of their lives, for the most part at least. This is why leadership, whether in the home, in business, or in government, must be very concerned how they govern.

Everyone under any leader will be affected by that leader. And the longer you or I are under any leader, we will become literal extensions and reflections, to some degree, of who is over us that we are feeding from. As we pointed out in the last chapter, you will always become like that which you submit to. There is no escaping this fact.
Every seed produces after its own kind. It has been this way since time immemorial. It is incapable of producing anything other than what it is intrinsically made of. And so, after so long, under the right conditions, you will begin to see the essence of that seed opening up for all to see. If you see a tree full of apples, don't let anyone tell you that it is an orange tree.

The fruit of a tree will always bear witness to what kind of tree it is. A good tree cannot bring forth bad fruit. And a bad tree cannot bring forth good fruit. Neither can an apple tree bring forth oranges. Nor can an orange tree bring forth apples. This same analogy can be applied to what is produced in the home or in society. If just rule was in the home where righteous principles were taught, then in that child you will be able to see this. And if the reverse is true, then that can be seen also.

This is not to say that someone, irrespective of how they were raised, will not deviate away from their foundational principles, but even if they do, you will still see fragments of their home training. However, through peer pressure, or youthful temptations and experimentation or whatnot, children will step outside of what they know they should not be doing. Once that child matures, they will hopefully return to their roots. Everyone knows basic right from wrong. All of the blame should never be on parents once they do their job as a parent.

So, when a child gets older and tests the limits of their freedoms, and it crosses lines that can get them in trouble, then that child has to bear the burden of their own actions. And in some cases, it is not a matter of bad parenting, but a matter of being influenced by and sucked into the gravitational pull of societal happenings.

What does any of this have to do with social justice and race relations? Well, let's look at the above from the perspective of government and its function. What burden does the government have in ensuring that those who are governed are governed with justice? What responsibility do leaders have when it comes to the ills of society? What is the government's role in ensuring every citizen is afforded all of the liberties and protections of any civilized society?

This chapter deals with the second leg of the concept of this book, rulership. Government exercises the greatest influence and control over the lives of its citizens. Much of what is happening in this country can be attributed to the failure of government, its complicity, or at worst, its direction [sic]. America's domestic policies are attributable for many of societies woes. Every nation has secrets. America does too.

How many times has this happened where the past ugly deeds of the government were made known? How many times have this country's secrets surfaced that happened twenty years ago? Too many times. This only means that it is possible that things are going on right now that we don't know anything about, things that will come to light sometime in the future.

I once read something that said that there are no accidents in politics. That if anything ever happened in politics, it was planned that way. It spoke of the high level of intelligence and wisdom of how governments operate. And occasionally, through the law of probability, you would think that something would accidentally go in our favor, but it seldom if ever does. That's because we are dealing with conscious and carefully planned governmental actions.

We have already dealt with the educational and religious systems in the last chapter. Now we want to bring to the forefront the political system that is also very much a part of these systems in America that are systemically racist. Now I want you to apply the same line of reasoning as before. If those who fashioned the political system have racial biases and prejudices against blacks, what kind of bent will that system have? What was the time period when the political and all other systems were erected in this country? What was the racial climate like? At the time these systems were formed, did slavery exist? Yes. So, what do you think the attitude of whites were about black people during this time period? Don't you think that this same attitude would be transferred over into and infused in these institutions? We made this point in chapter two. We all know the answers to these questions. So why is it so hard to face the facts?

These things are not merely relics of the past. You cannot separate what happened yesterday from what is happening today. The past is inextricably tied to the present. And what we do presently will be inextricably tied to the future. As it is with individuals, so it is with governments. We said these things won't be comfortable to talk about. How could they be? No one wants their faults pointed out. Who does? But you should never call anyone who points these things out unpatriotic. What greater love can one have for their country than wanting her to be better?

You mean to tell me you never had to tell someone who you loved that they were wrong about something? Why did you feel you had to point their wrongs out? Was it easy? Did it mean you loved them any less? And more importantly, what happened afterwards, did it begin the healing process?

Sometimes you have to hurt what you love to make it better. Doctors are known to break bones to reset them. That intentional pain that was inflicted corrected a deformity. What is deformity? An imperfection. A blemish? Something that is marred. Is America perfect? Does she have any blemishes? Is the face of America marred with her past and present mistreatment of blacks?

You have people in this country who sit on both sides of the race issue. Some want change. Some want to make things right so the nation can move forward. Others know what the truth is, but don't want change. They are resistant to any kind of change. They could care less about what happened in the past. They are proud of their historical roots as enslavers.

They have the same attitudes that their forefathers had who owned slaves. Is this true or is this false? If you can show me I'm lying then I will shut up and you can discard everything mentioned in this book. But you won't be able to because you know I'm right. Racism in this country is actively present in the hearts and minds of a certain segment of the white community.

America is a divided nation. The gap that exists between the views of the far right and the views of the far left seems unbridgeable. Even on the most pivotal of issues, including the race issue, common ground can't be reached. Any deals that are reached on any significant agenda items involves some form of personal or professional gain instead of the welfare of the nation or the constituents that these elected officials represent.

Such was the case with the third stimulus package prior to Donald Trump's departure from the White House. Politics were put above the real suffering that people were going through. People in Washington have bigger agendas. You and I are never at the top of their list of priorities.

Good leadership is leadership that leads with the people they are leading in the forefront of their minds. They don't do things for self-aggrandizement. When you can put the people first, your leadership is secure. But when you fleece the people then your rule will soon come to an end by the very people you are supposed to represent.

I'll give you that in this package if you add this with it or give me this in that one. If that kind of bargaining is for that senator's or that representative's constituents, then that kind of political maneuvering and negotiating is necessary to get your agenda across.

However, this is not always the case. Often, other interests are involved. This is why you have these lobbyist groups vying for and backing certain candidates and political officials that will support their interests and not the interests of the people. Most of these interests are connected with the rich, multinational corporations, or big banking institutions.

When you say that the government is of the people, for the people, and by the people, I find that extremely hard to believe. If the government was really for the people, then so many would not have to subsist on the bare necessities of life. So many would not be railroaded in the courts. So many would not be homeless or jobless. And so many would be able to depend on the government for the redress of their grievances. You can tell a lot about a government by the condition of its people. And if the condition of the people is the measure of government, then the condition of the American people speaks volumes.

The template for government was laid down by Jesus when he said that it matters not if you do everything good for those who really don't need it, he was speaking of himself; but what really matters is what you do for the little people. Those who are most in need should be able to depend on government to help them get through rough times. Not that this should be a welfare state where there is complete dependence on the part of many who, for whatever reason, won't do anything to become self-sufficient. Government should not have to carry the burden of those who are capable to work but refuse to work.

But when governments fail in its duty to the people, what are the effects? Should the government be held responsible at all like some parents are? What should be the price of nonfeasance by those in government? What does the Declaration of Independence say about when governments are destructive of just ends? Doesn't it say that the people have a right to alter or abolish it? These are not my words. These are the words of the founding fathers that you will be able to read in their entirety in the concluding chapters of this book.

In the preamble to the United States Constitution, you find these words; 'We the people hold these truths to be self-evident, that all Men are created equal, that they are endowed by their Creator with certain unalienable Rights, that among these are Life, Liberty, and the Pursuit of Happiness.

Ask yourself, has the government treated you as an equal? What are the unalienable rights you are endowed with by the Creator? Have those rights been recognized, or have you been deprived of those rights in any way? What is life? And how does liberty and the pursuit of happiness tie into it?

Black people have never been a part of the 'We' in 'We the people.'. Blacks most definitely were not seen as an equal to whites. The rights that we have been endowed with by our Creator has not been recognized by you as being worthy enough not to be infringed upon. We have the God-given right to have the pathway that leads to the fulfillment of our needs unimpeded. As a government, you have failed in that regard. The first law of life is freedom. Real freedom is being unrestricted in your life to pursue the happiness that all life has an innate desire and need for, and to enjoy what you have been endowed with by your Creator. This is the connection between life, liberty, and the pursuit of happiness.

Question; why should happiness in life have to be pursued? Why has happiness been so elusive that you would have to pursue it in the first place? Why does it seem like attaining real happiness is like a false hope that keeps that promise beyond reach?

Happiness is an essential need that most of us have never experienced. And as a result, we live unfulfilled lives. Real happiness is enduring and perpetual. Not this fleeting stuff we get from acts that bring us temporary fulfillment, and sometimes pain and regret too. So, we live our whole lives always chasing this elusive state of happiness.

In the home, happiness is something that should not have to be pursued. Happiness should be a byproduct of a loving home environment because mommy and daddy makes sure that the atmosphere in the home is peaceful, loving, and suitable to making sure that the children enjoyed their upbringing and ultimately their life beyond home. If not, they can be expected to look for, or pursue happiness elsewhere. This is commonplace when the needs of the child are not met at home, they go outside the home to fulfill a need or desire they have.

What is real happiness and how can it be attained? If happiness is defined as a state of wellbeing and contentment, joy, or a pleasurable or satisfying experience; are you happy? Can someone be happy if they are not treated right? No. Can someone be happy if they don't understand life or their purpose in life? No. So when happiness can't be found in the home, then alternative forms of happiness are pursued. Forms that are temporary and carry with them things that are not good.

Real happiness can't be found in a bottle. It can't be found in a pill. Or in any mind-altering substance. Your pleasure centers in your brain may allow you to experience a certain high, but when you come down, your reality remains. Your condition is unchanged. The madness in the world has not gone anywhere. Nor can real happiness be found in non-fulfilling uncommitted relationships.

Did you know that the best way to get something accomplished that you don't want others to know about is to keep them occupied and distracted with things that feeds a weakness or a low desire in them? By keeping the minds of the people focused on frivolous things, you can take care of your business without it ever being noticed.

I'm not against having a good time. But what does that mean? Is having a good time hanging out in the streets or clubs dancing, drinking, and then sleeping around? If this is your idea of fun, then no wonder why it is so easy for those in power to get away with their crap because no one is sober minded enough to really pay attention to what is happening.

The pursuit of happiness in America is like chasing a shadow that gets further away from you the closer you try to reach it. Happiness, true happiness, is found in having a pleasing relationship with your Creator who is the Most High. That relationship can elevate your entire being to heights that no drug could ever take you. You should never look to government as the source of your happiness, but it is reasonable to expect government not to interfere with your pursuit of happiness by depriving you of your inalienable rights that they acknowledge are endowed upon you by your Creator.

It is hard to imagine how anyone can take delight in the pain and suffering of others. Someone would have to be really cold hearted and indifferent to rule as mercilessly as many of those are who rule this nation seem to be when it comes to the needs of many of its citizens. This kind of detachment makes it easy to make decisions that can either cause mass suffering or ignore mass suffering. Anyone who is not in their socioeconomic class is subject to being victimized, including poor whites. Someone has to be the fodder to feed the system that keeps the engine of America running.

The only power government has is by the consent of the governed. The government is not the real power. The real power is in the people. And the power of the people is in our unity. The power of the people is being as knowledgeable of our rights and securing those rights through the most appropriate and effective means possible.

Remember, an organized lie is more effective than disorganized truth. Being scattered in different groups and organizations is not necessarily bad because we are able to meet the many different needs of our people. At the same time, there needs to be a time when we all must come together as a whole to be more effective.

Never forget the golden rule of governing and being governed, which is to, do unto others as you want done unto you.

6_ Tricks, Lies, and Deceit

It is necessary, in my opinion, to devote an entire chapter to lies, their effect, and those who tell them. And ultimately to the truth, its effect, and those who speak it. In truth, and let's be honest now, do you think it is wise to expect someone who does not treat you right to teach you right? The odds of that happening is slim to none.

When someone has put a system in place to keep you subjugated, exposing the truth of that system will unravel all of the inner workings and intricacies of that system will lead to its undoing. This world is built on lies and falsehoods and on the backs of the suffering masses. Keeping us enshrouded in darkness or in a state of ignorance is their protection from detection. The prevalence of deception is so widespread and pervasive that it is hardly noticeable because it has become so enmeshed into the fabric of society. It is blended in so seamlessly that it is virtually undetectable. This fact embodies just how powerful and effective these systems have been.

The propaganda machine plays a key role in churning out lies and misinformation, and then making sure that the truth is not allowed to have access to the same platform. It takes someone embodied with and emboldened by the truth or one who has an exceptional ability to see through lies to expose them. This is something that everyone is not qualified to do.

The people's senses are literally bombarded day and night with false narratives that are designed to color the perception of those who are easily susceptible to being influenced in any direction the puppeteers want them to go. Many that are the face of these massive lie campaigns are being used to further the aims of the satanic elite. Some knowingly, others not. Mass manipulation is definitely afoot. It has been in play since the inception of this world, and it looks like it won't be ending anytime soon.

Because of the inherent blinding power in tricks, lies, and deceit, the people are rendered handicapped when it comes to being able to take basic ordinary steps to protect themselves from the poison that is contained in lies and those who spew them.

Some people lie so much and so naturally that it seems as if the lie was built right into their nature. It takes no effort at all for them to lie. They have no conscience to contend with. It's like they were born to be an agent and conveyor of lies.

It is hard for most people to believe that such a trait exists in human beings where a lie is built into their nature. You say that people can't be that inherently wicked. This denial is what keeps the liar safe and his lie from being exposed. Lies are dangerous because anyone who accepts a lie as the truth will not only live their life according to that lie, but they will pass that lie on down to their children. And they will pass it on to theirs until it becomes so cyclical that the liar can sit back and watch is handiwork without having to do anything. These are generational falsehoods.

When someone comes along and exposes the lie for what it is, the people have all sorts of visceral reactions. This stems from the system of lies that has programmed them to reject the truth. Lies have become a huge part of our diet. The truth is like having a child sitting at the dinner table being told that he has to sit there until he eats his vegetables. You know they are good for you but you refuse to eat them anyway.

Unless you are conscious and have a strong desire to be mentally healthy, then you too will refuse something that will improve your mental, moral, and spiritual health, in the same way a child will stubbornly refuse to eat his vegetables that will improve his physical health. Foods that are the best for us to eat are generally not the tastiest, but they are better for us. Truth is not always easy to hear or live by, but it is better for us. Being raised with lies instead of truth is like being raised not having healthy food as a part of your diet. So when you get older it takes being aware of the health benefits associated with healthy eating to get people to change their diets. Or unless some health scare forces them to eat better.

Today there are people who cut certain foods out of their diet for various personal reasons. When you have the knowledge of the science of healthy versus unhealthy food, this allows you to make enlightened choices when it comes to what you put in your body. Having the knowledge of the science of truth versus a lie allows you to do the same. Then you have the other group who no matter how much they are made aware of the difference between food that is good for them verses food that is not, they refuse to let go of certain eating habits no matter how bad or disease causing the food is.

Some because they lack the willpower. Others because they simply don't care. And then you have those who reason that this type of food and eating has been in their family for years. And if big momma says it's okay to eat, then I'm gone go with what she says over what anybody else has to say. I'm sorry to say this, and I mean no disrespect, but there is a degree of ignorance in that argument. How many things did you do growing up because of how you were raised that you no longer do now that you are grown?

What did you believe in growing up that has since been replaced by another belief? If you come into the knowledge of something different, better, or greater, is it not wise to put away something you did yesterday if you have a better understanding of it today even if it is tied to family tradition?

My mother and I don't agree on everything. This does not make us love each other any less. We accept that we have our own thoughts and opinions when it comes to certain things and we leave it at that.

All of us won't agree on every single thing. We shouldn't be expected to. At the same time, we can't afford to let our differences of opinion, which are small and insignificant when compared to the bigger picture, to come between us or our focus in changing the landscape of how justice is given to some and not to all.

Our condition beckons us to seek the underlying reasons that give rise to what we go through. I emphasize underlying because we already know the surface reasons. The issue is more than what meets the eye. What we presently know and rely on is not enough for us to be able to fully grasp the condition that lies contribute to.

There is an undercurrent of tricks, lies, and deceit that is at the root of much of the madness surrounding our lives. Don't be upset with the one who exposes the lie or the liar.
Instead, we should find solace and comfort in knowing that someone has the courage to speak truth to power with the force of strength and wisdom on our behalf without any fear of consequences. When the cloak of fear is removed, you are able to challenge the powers of this world with a spirit that is considered superhuman to the average person. If you are not ye like this then support those who are.

Lies are poisonous. They cause sickness to those who ingest them destroying them from the inside out. You look like a man or a woman on the outside, but that which makes you that on the inside is gone. This sickness has metastasized to the point that it has affected everyone within the sphere of its touch.
The only curative agent to heal this sickness is truth. Without truth to serve as the remedial solution, we will continue to suffer in our ignorance. Such is the therapeutic power of truth to counter lies. I repeat, truth is the only curative agent that can heal a mind that has been made weak and sick by feeding on lies.

Either through omission or outright lying, the effect of a lie is the same. Lies, when you take them for truth can cause irreparable damage. Damage that can't be easily undone. How many times have you acted on a lie only to find out later that you were wrong? How many times was someone convicted of a crime on the basis of a lie only to find out later they were actually innocent?

This has happened way too many times. This is why knowing the truth is important. You are more informed, you will make less mistakes, you won't be as easily deceived, and everyone is better off as a result, except the liar that is. We have to become humble enough to know that we don't know it all. That maybe someone else has the answer or solution to what we don't know. We can't afford to let false pride or ego get in the way of listening to others who may have the understanding to what is so perplexing to so many of us.

Arrogance has no place among us when we need each other's invaluable input. No one individual can take up the mantle to fight against the forces that are arrayed against us. It will take a collective united organized front. I want to make this clear for the record, you and I have to take responsibility for our own actions that have contributed to our condition. I will take this up when we get to Black on Black violence which has become a scourge in our communities.

In this book I'm focused on hidden forces that have put the state of racism in this country on the seemingly unending course that it is on. Once something is initiated, you can put it together in such a way that it will function automatically with no outside interference. This is what a system does. And this is what is being attacked. Systems. Not individuals. Causes. Not effects.

Pathologists study the origin and causes of diseases. This study and understanding is important in not only diagnosing diseases, but in their prevention and treatment. The answer to a health problem should not always be found in a pill. Pills only treat effects. Exercising willpower is a more healthier option if your condition does not demand a pill as the only solution. The ultimate objective is to treat the root cause of our condition and not the effect of what a root cause produced. The latter is the weaker approach and is the path of least resistance and will only keep the cycle of poverty, violence, ignorance, bad health, injustice, and inequality going.

Most disease causing organisms are microscopic. Lies are too. It would be nice if someone's nose grew like Pinocchio every time they told a lie. That is not how it works. If that were the case, then some people's noses would be a mile long.
Pinocchio is a fairytale. A hyperbolic expression. One that paints a grim picture of a reality that lies are not easy to detect although in the fairytale it suggests otherwise.
It is written in the Holy Bible that, "There is a way which seems right to a man, but the ends thereof are the ways of death.". My question is how can something that is so wrong be made to seem so right? How can death be dressed up to look like life? When something can be given the

THE HAND THAT ROCKS THE CRADLE

impression of being one thing when it is the exact opposite is the work of a master deceiver.

How good do you have to be to take something that is bad for somebody and make it look good? A liar knows the nature of you and can reach you right through your nature. But we can't see the subtlety at play. It almost reminds me of the show, The Carbonaro Effect. The host of the show works all kinds of mind blowing magic tricks on unsuspecting people. And no matter how outlandish his act is, even right before their very eyes, they buy into things that flies in the face of reason, logic, and physics. They accept fantasy for reality in even the most bizarre scenarios.

Could this be why our lifestyles are really death styles? We are killing ourselves and don't even know why. When we live our lives on the guidance of a master manipulator who constructed a world that is diametrically opposed to our natures, this leads to an untimely death. "My people", God speaking, "are destroyed for the lack of knowledge.". Jesus said that you shall know the truth, and although you don't know it now, there will come a time when there will be a truth from me that is so powerful that it will free you.

Free you from what or from who? A truth that will free you from all the things that a lie has made you a slave to. Free you from a state of ignorance. And free you from the influence and control of the liar whose time is up. There will come a time when this truth will be made known to you by the one I send to you. You will know him by his works as much as by his words.

All you have to do is watch and listen intently. And for those who have eyes to see, it will be so obvious and clear that there is a truth being spoken that lines up with the scriptures and the time we are living in. And guess what, he won't be sent to you by your oppressor.

As we bring this chapter to a close, I hope that it has been made abundantly clear the level of deception that we are up against. Don't let anyone's words stand on its own merit. No one is beyond deceiving you. And no one is immune from being deceived in this world.

You can't tell a person who has a 'watch on' what time it is. A 'watch on' is being able to observe your condition and surroundings and use that observation to calculate things to render an understanding of the time. Once you know what time it is, no one will ever be able to get over on you. And all the smoke and mirrors won't be able to distract you. However, if you can't read the time on your own, then you have to rely on someone who knows what time it is. Some wise people know the time, but are unwillingly to share what they know. Then the ones who do share what they know are attacked by the ones who really don't want you to know.

And sadly, if the truth comes from someone who looks like you, you sometimes don't accept it. This is part of the sickness we suffer from. We don't think too highly of ourselves to think that someone black can be right about something. Deception can not only make wrong look right, but it can also make right look wrong.

An example of this can be encapsulated in the following exchange I once read about. The story as I recall it went like this, 'there was a Black woman on a train on her way from, let's say, Detroit to Chicago. On the train, at some point during the trip, she saw a black porter and asked him how much longer will it be until they arrived in Chicago? He told her that it will be about two more hours. And no sooner after he told her this as he was walking away she asked the same question to a white attendant on the train. He told her the same thing the black porter told her, about two hours. The porter overheard her asking the white attendant the same question she just asked him and came back and asked her why did she have to ask the attendant what she just asked him? She said that she had to get it in black and white.'.

This was a lighthearted way of exposing a real problem with us as a people. We are so trusting of those who have a long history of lying to us, and we are so hesitant to believe what someone of our own race has to say. This is something deeply embedded within the psyche of our people. This goes back to those two complexes mentioned in an earlier chapter; superiority complex and inferiority complex.

We have been programmed to trust only white and to distrust ourselves. This is the workings of the scientific way of dividing us against one another through the implementation of Willie Lynch's so-called foolproof plan on how to control and get the most out of slaves. In many ways he was the architect behind the science of how to divide and conquer an entire people by focusing on specific differences. And highlighting those differences all out of proportion. Those differences live on to this very day.

One of the effects that was an outgrowth from those differences focused on having slaves trust only white people. Invariably, being psychologically conditioned to trust only whites, it would cause us to distrust one another. How many times have we been so quick to believe someone white who says something that a Black person has been saying for years?

This hesitancy stems from being made to think so little of ourselves. Unless and until someone white authenticates what the black person says we will be hesitant to believe in our own people. But once white America gives her stamp of approval, then it must be true, right, or okay, and thus, safe to fully accept or believe. Like we said, any person can deceive you. Black or white. So, just because someone black says something we still have to search out the truth of what they are saying. Satan deceived the whole world. Who knows who has been stung by his poison? Who knows if the Black person who is put out front is being used to garner the support and gain the trust of black people who won't buy into something if it comes from someone white?

Some blacks allow themselves to be used as tools for white people to convey their ideas to facilitate their agenda. Be careful. Approach matters with caution. Lying tongues are everywhere. The lie that there is no racism in this country and in the institutions that undergird it is one of the biggest lies out right now. You believe what you want and who you want, you have that right. But if you put your trust and confidence in something that is a lie or in someone who is a liar, then you have to live with the consequences of believing in a lie, especially if the truth has been presented to expose and counter the lie.

7_ Criminal Justice Reform

I want to be as detailed as possible because there is much talk about criminal justice reform, but as of the date of this writing there has been more talk than any meaningful action. Or what has been proposed and changed is only a surface reformation that has not made a real dent in mass incarceration, especially on the state level. This cause has been championed by many. Their efforts must be applauded. Any progress beats no progress. Yet, there is so much more that needs to be done in order to curb crime and end mass incarceration.

Law and order should and must govern society. Those who don't comport themselves to the rule of law subject themselves to being removed from a society based on law. However, when conditions have been manufactured and law is used as a cover to corral the undesirables so that they become the fuel to keep a massive slave enterprise going, and then the less threatening of these menaces are thrown right back into conditions only to be recaught at a later time to be recycled, is a process that must end.

This catch and release system is an unending cycle that bodes no one well except those who are the real profiteers of crime.

Two Michigan legislatures came to Muskegon Correctional Facility to give us updates on what was going on in Lansing, the state Capitol, dealing with prison reform. One of them said that in politics, things move at a galatial pace when it comes to getting certain legislative agenda items accomplished.

I suppose this is true when the legislative items being proposed or worked on are not particularly important to them or what is being proposed is not very popular or is a hot-button issue. And that to go forward with some issues may carry with it some form of political blowback. Politics is very often put above the right or the humane thing to do. Effective change can happen and at a more accelerated pace if the issue is important enough. This just points to the fact that some or most are not really in favor of making any significant changes across the board on criminal justice reform while knowing the justice system is flawed.

If the system wasn't flawed, then there would not be such a big disparity in how lopsided time is doled out between blacks and whites. Or even in the rates of incarceration between blacks and whites. Unless of course you think Black people are more prone to criminality than whites. We have already highlighted and explained the state of mind of white supremacy which embodies the idea of white rule and white dominance. There are many whites in every professional field that hold this idea of white rule over everyone else as a core belief.

What about the medical field? How does this mindset effect patients who are not white when treated by white doctors? What about banking and other lending institutions? How does this mindset effect those who are not white when the lenders are white? What about those who legislate? If a legislature is in any way biased, racist, or prejudiced against black and brown folks, then do you think that that mindset can have a negative effect on those who are not white and in favor of whites?

These are merely rhetorical questions that require no answer. They are for you to consider so that you don't move away from the thought that if someone is in a position of power to adversely affect the lives of those who are not white, will they? Have they?

Now what about judges, prosecutors, and even defense attorneys? If the criminal justice system is tainted by racism then this accounts for the great disparity not only in sentencing, but in what charges are filed, in what plea deals are offered, and the overall way in which the case is tried and prosecuted.

This explains why certain laws favor whites. This results in blacks being overcharged, given higher bails, and longer sentences. This is carried over into the appeals process mentioned as well. What do the numbers say about who is given relief from judgment? By the numbers, who is generally resentenced, retried, or released? It is more than evident and abundantly clear that the criminal justice system needs overhauling. On both the state and federal level. There needs to be honest and clear dialogue about the particular aspects of this system that needs to be reformed.

There are things that needs to be added, and other parts that needs to be completely done away with. Below are just a few reforms to be given serious thought to if lawmakers are serious about criminal justice reform. These suggestions reflect the state of Michigan's criminal justice system and its laws in particular:

* Laws and statutes need to reflect that which is fundamentally fair.

* Sentencing guidelines need to be proportionate to the alleged offense and overall circumstances.

* Do away with sentence enhancers because they largely target and are apt to be applicable to Black and Brown people.

* Make vocational training applicable to everyone and not just those who have early release dates (E.R.D.'s).

* Cap life sentences to a fixed number of years instead of natural life sentences which are essentially death sentences, except in rare and exceptional cases.

* Abolish the felony murder doctrine completely, especially the idea of holding aiders and abettors without the means necessary for murder from being culpable for the principal's actions or state of mind.

* Consider for release those who age out of crime after a certain age and number of years served.

* Incentivize good behavior to earn credit towards sentence reduction or disciplinary credits.

* End mandatory minimum sentencing which strips judges of discretionary sentencing when extenuating circumstances call for it.

* Adopt reform measures from other states that have proven to be effective in those states.

Now I would like for us to look at the concept of crime from a particular angle that we may have never considered. I will do this by way of quoting Dr. Martin Luther King Jr in a speech he delivered to The Southern Christian Leadership Conference on August 15, 1967, in Atlanta when he gave his insight and analysis on social disorder and laid out a plan of action against poverty, discrimination, and racism. The following are his words:

"A million words will be written and spoken to discuss the ghetto outbreaks, but for a perceptive and vivid expression of culpability I would like to submit two sentences written a century ago by Victor Hugo; "If the soul is left in darkness, sins will be committed. The guilty one is not he who commits the sin, but he who causes the darkness.".

The policymakers of the white society have caused the darkness; they created discrimination; they created slums; they perpetuated unemployment, ignorance, and poverty. It is incontestable and deplorable that Negroes have committed crimes, but they are derivative crimes.". What exactly is a derivative crime? Dr. King goes on to say, "These crimes are born of the greater crimes of the white society. So when we ask Negroes to abide by the law, let us also declare that the White man does not abide by law in the ghettos. Day in and day out he violates welfare laws to deprive the poor of their meager allotments; he flagrantly violates building codes and regulations; his police make a mockery of law; he violates laws on equal employment and education and the provisions for civil services. The slums are the handiwork of a vicious system of the White society; Negroes live in them but do not make them any more than a prisoner makes a prison...' ".

He went on to say, "Let us say boldly that if the total slum violations of law by the White man over the years were calculated and compared with the law-breaking of a few days of riots, the hardened criminal would be the White man." .There is more but our point has been made by introducing the term 'derivative crime'. I thought that that was a very insightful explanation of some of the reasons blacks engage in criminal activity. I didn't say excuse because there is no excuse for it, but there are reasons why. Conditions exist that precipitate the commission of crimes. Whoever controls those conditions, controls the commission of crimes.

So please don't take this quote or this line of reasoning out of context. Again, I'm not making any excuses for lawless behavior, I'm giving a reason for it as seen by Martin Luther King Jr. I'm using an argument that I think needs to be taken under critical analysis as part of the underlying reasons why many crimes are committed in and by those in black communities. If you really want to dig deep into prison reform, which starts with crime prevention, then it behooves you not to gloss over this point. Everything starts at the top and trickles down. The more we focus on the effect of crime rather than its causes, then we won't be as effective as we could be in putting a real dent in crime.

A derivative crime derives from the concept that a previously committed crime by one person or people facilitates or is a cause of a future crime committed by another person or people. A simplistic way of looking at this is recognizing that one thing leads to another.

A deeper more penetrating view involves understanding the science of how the law of cause and effect works. When you can work this law, it will make you a master of outcomes. If you initiate or cause a certain happening, then it logically follows that it will produce an effect that is the direct result of what you initiated or caused beforehand. And when you can control what you cause, you can control or predict the effect of what you cause.

Human nature, when studied, can be manipulated. Whenever you deprive a human being of an essential element it needs for its stability, it will find ways to compensate for what is missing. This is a natural occurrence. This happens in nature and in our nature. When you know how to keep a very specific need away from someone, then a very specific response can be predicted with almost pinpoint accuracy. Naturally of course. And no one will be the wiser.

When you have this ability, you can see criminal actions taking place in the future by those deprived of certain necessities and create a foothold in certain industries to capitalize on what you know is coming. If that ain't criminal then I don't know what is.

So, what crime or crimes have been committed by someone and what other crime or crimes were committed by another? One of the most violent crimes that can be committed is to create a condition of poverty. The war on poverty is a violent tactical assault that is not intended to root out poverty but to create a condition that serves as the seminal fluid to spawn a host of other conditions.

Conditions that create a domino effect and produces a vicious cycle for millions of black, brown, and poor whites to live in and suffer through. Poverty is a crime against humanity. It is a capital offense and should have no statute of limitations to bring the perpetrators to justice. The government's hand in this cannot be ignored. The government is the hand that rocks the cradle of society.

Those who rock the cradle are responsible because they control, by purposefully molding a society that reflects a wickedly wise attempt to keep blacks in a perpetual state of slavery by using advanced and sophisticated techniques. The industry of slavery, like any other industry, has to constantly be retooled to keep pace with the changing times. Ask yourself, are Black people completely free? Or are blacks still subject to and under the control white America? This may be hard to swallow for some I know. But some of you will be able to relate to this.

Others will not. I'm okay with that. My job is not to force anything on you or to try to convince you of anything. I'm giving it to you the way I see it. Let me ask you this, have you ever wondered why there is so much resistance to the people's cry and demand for basic liberties? What prevents America from doing the right thing? Does she fear losing something? Is she hiding something? Or could it be that she is protecting something? If white supremacy is real, and it is, then you better believe that a system has been put in place for its permanence. And it may have to be upgraded, tweaked, or calibrated from time to time to keep it effectively intact.

Let's cut to the chase. What I'm proposing is that you are crooked and rotten to the core and that your actions, although cleverly concealed, makes you the principal, aider and abettor, and accessory after the fact of crimes that have caused others to be unwittingly complicit in their own demise. You are a master criminal who has masterminded the most elaborate, the most heinous, and the most effective criminal enterprise the world has ever known. You should be charged with RICO (Racketeer Influenced and Corrupt Organizations [Act]) for running a continuing criminal enterprise from which you profit from to this very day.

Reform should start with you. But can you be reformed? Do you even care to be? Your hand in creating the darkness has to be acknowledged. Let's not lose sight of the profundity in the statement made by Victor Hugo; "If the soul is left in darkness, sins will be committed. The guilty one is not he who commits the sin, but he who causes the darkness.". How much better can it be said than that? Do you take issue with being called a criminal? Does this upset you? My aim is not to taunt you. I'm merely confronting you with the truth of yourself. You may not like it, but is it the truth or is it a lie?

Martin Luther King Jr. called you a hardened criminal. He recognized your involvement in creating the slums that would facilitate a high likelihood of criminal behavior by those in such conditions. But you love him. You honor him. But if he were alive today speaking like that you would take issue with that. Any of our leaders that you don't like you do everything you can do to marginalize them. To turn their own people against them. And upon their deaths, you resurrect them. At your leisure of course. And in a manner that suits you. You did it with Malcolm X. You couldn't stand him when he was alive, not even the sight of him. But now he is accepted by you because you don't fear the dead, only the living. So now you give us a sanitized version of Malcolm X.

You may say what does this have to do with criminal justice reform? Plenty. You have been charged with creating and keeping Black people in darkness. And any leader with the light of knowledge that is good for us, is bad for you because it exposes you, so you do everything in your power to extinguish that light. By keeping us ignorant, you are free to carry on with your vast criminal enterprise undetected and uninterrupted. I think you are the pot calling the kettle black by your vilification of criminals and criminality when you engage in criminal conduct more than anyone else on the planet. When you do this you are exhibiting the epitome of hypocrisy. You have committed the most egregious crimes imaginable. And they are not your garden-variety crimes either. Your crimes do not just effect individuals, but entire peoples and nations.

TERRY TRIGGS

What have you done? You have engaged in wholesale kidnapping, murder, rape, identity theft, etc., and to this day you continue to rob people of the freedom to grow into their full potential by your continued injustice and denial of equality of opportunity. These are criminal acts. I want to get back to criminal justice reform from another vantage point, that if fixed, it could be the fulcrum to provide some balance where imbalance presently exists. The jury system or jury selection process whose final composition does not adequately reflect a fair cross section of the community, is, I think, an impediment to real justice.
Let's be truthful, if there is no one sitting on the jury that has no way of identifying with a defendant on trial, not from a criminalistic standpoint, but as far as racial identity, then this can lead to the denial of a just verdict.

The fact of the matter is that black people and white people assess race differently. It shouldn't make a difference but it does make a difference when the perpetrator of a crime is black or white and the victim is black or white. No racial identity exists when there is a black defendant on trial and the victim is white and there is an all-white jury weighing the facts and judging the case. This creates a problem. The same dilemma is present when there is a white defendant, a black victim, and an all-white jury. What about when there is a black defendant, black victim, and all white jury. Does the jury give more empathy when they are the same race as the victim? Or less empathy when the victim is not of their race? What kinds of discussions are a part of or kept out of

96

the deliberation process when the make-up of the jury is lacking views and insights from a broader base?

Now what if we expanded our scenarios to include black or white witnesses and the various construction or make-up of potential jurors? Let's get Mr. Van Dykes take on it.

"A white juror sitting in a jury box listening to the testimony of a black witness would sift and evaluate and appraise that testimony through a screen of preconceived notions about what black people are...The black juror, because of more similar life experiences to the black witness would appraise that testimony from a distinctively different vantage point...". This taken from Jury Selection Procedures; by Jon M. Van Dyke (1977).further,

"Black and white jurors assess guilt differently when the defendant or victim is black...the absence of racial identity between defendant and those excluded also has been noted by judges denying that such a risk exists. Several courts have suggested that the risk of prejudice from jury discrimination error is especially high when blacks are excluded from juries that judge Black defendants accused of a crime against white victims." Michigan Law Review pg. 81

For context purposes I will share the following: I was involved in a robbery that turned deadly when I was twenty years old. I am fifty-two now. I am Black. The victims in my case were white. I had an all-white jury. Result. Guilty of two counts of Felony Murder.

Despite not having killed anyone myself, the way the felony murder law is constructed, it makes or allows for all participants to be held equally culpable.

This dynamic is seen every day in the criminal justice system. This is why many blacks see ourselves as being railroaded in the criminal justice system and that the courts are places where modern lynchings take place under the pretense of justice. If there is no reform in critical areas such as this, then the wheel of injustice will keep turning.

I want to share a perspective from a white judge ruling on the below case wherein he stated that,

"Were it not for the perceived likelihood that jurors will favor defendants of their own class, there would be no reason to suppose that a jury selection process that systematically excluded persons of a certain race would be the basis of any legitimate complaint by criminal defendants of that race.". 430 U.S. 482, 516 (1970).

When you can identify with someone you are able to relate to things about that person that others are unable to. And this is why I said earlier in reference to the killings taking place by white police officers against black people that if this problem landed at the doorstep of white folks then they would be more inclined to take notice and take action. Wouldn't you see a problem differently and be effected by it differently if it was more closer to home? We can't ignore the differences that exists between the races. We are all human beings, yet we are wired differently.

I would like to quote something else taken from the Michigan Law Journal by another white jurist who recognized the many differences between different people and why distinctive factors should be considered and taken into account;

"Different social groups have different and distinct individual personalities, attitudes, motivations, and behavioral influences that influences their thinking and actions. This is even true with different people within the same social group; but even more so when you have different people in different groups.".

How broad a perspective is that in explaining the vast differences that exists naturally between different people? I think that is a good description of why there needs to be an emphasis on diverse representation in many areas and on many platforms. This diversity is needed not only in law, but in the worlds of education, economics, religion, politics, and so on. When you have a healthy mix of qualified individuals across all racial backgrounds and ethnic lines, then their involvement within these different areas would be pivotal in rectifying some of the injustices that presently exist.

Politicians are clock milkers. They take something that takes a relatively short amount of time to accomplish and stretch it out for months and years. Some things could be changed more quickly if the straight line method was used.

Criminal justice reform can happen with the snap of a finger, but it is being dragged out for reasons that correspond with what we shared in earlier chapters. To upend the criminal justice in its present state is like disrupting a well-balanced ecosystem.

I will close with a quote from The Sentencing Project; *"The particular drivers of disparity may be related to policy, offending, implicit bias, or some combination. Regardless of the causes, however, the simple fact of these disparities should be disturbing given the consequences for individuals and communities...*

...one has to wonder whether there would have been more of an urgency to understand and remedy the disparity directly had the ratios been reversed. While chronic racial and ethnic disparity in imprisonment has been a known feature of the prison system for many decades, there has been relatively little serious consideration of adjustments that can be made --- inside or outside the justice system --- toward changing this pattern.".

Many books have been written about crime and its causes, Their views to me are archaic and don't go deep enough. They only deal with surface or cosmetic reasons for the causes of crime. While at the same time acknowledging that there are social and psychological factors which lead to the commission of crimes.

My question would be this; why would you discount social and psychological factors in assessing criminal behavior patterns?

By your own admission, you know why, even if you don't use the term systemic racism, you indirectly point to a primary cause that creates the conditions that leads to criminal activity. It is not whether or not criminal justice reform is needed. It's a matter of when and how comprehensive the reform will be when those reforms are made.

8_ The Prison Industrial Complex

The Prison Industrial Complex in America is one of the biggest human rights violations in the world. I'm not referring to the concept of imprisonment to punish offenders to keep society safe, or to curtail crime, that is wholly understandable. But when your intent and purpose is centered around profit, legalized slave labor, and genocide through mass incarceration, then you have put a dollar amount, inhumane treatment, and your disregard for human life over a tool that should be used to deter crime through a system of legitimate jurisprudence.

If you have never been incarcerated, no amount of explaining will give you the complete understanding of what it is like to be in prison serving time, hard or otherwise. I know they say that you can't judge a person or understand them until you walk in their shoes. But I'm here to tell you that there is no shoe that you can put on that will help you see, hear, smell, feel, and experience the rigors of confinement. The best way that I can describe prison is that it is a beast on another level. And the only way you won't feel the natural effects of this unnatural environment is if you are somehow mentally anesthetized. It took about ten years for my anesthesia to wear off.

Since then I have felt every prick, prod, and poke of my prison experience. Some of my experiences and views will be shared in this chapter that tie into the theme of this book on social justice and race relations. The prison system varies from state to state. And in each state, the prison experience is different in different prison settings depending on the level of confinement you are housed in.

In Michigan, this classification is based upon mainly two factors, the amount of time you are serving and your management level. Within this mix, some prisons are more relaxed, while others are powder kegs. One thing they all have in common however is the disproportionate number of blacks locked up in comparison to whites in relation to the percentage these groups are populated in society.

Something is wrong when black people make up roughly approximately 13% of the population in society. And out of that 13%, Black male men make up roughly less than half of that. Combine that with the fact that black men are locked up at a 80% higher rate than whites with a national average of 5.1:1. My question is this, are black men born criminals? Are we prone to criminality more than any other racial or ethnic group? Or are we, as Victor Hugo said, a soul left in darkness destined to commit sinful acts as a result?

The prison industrial complex in America is a reflection of what kind of nation she is no matter how she shows herself off to be before the world. She is like that shiny plastic arrangement of fake fruit you put on display for decoration purposes only? Oh how that fruit is so beautiful outwardly, but inwardly it is hollow and devoid of that which makes it real fruit. If America is so good and so right then why are more people locked up for committing crime than anywhere else in the world?

This is America. She touts herself as this beacon of light, but she is as dark as a moonless night. She is hollow on the inside. America lacks the human decency necessary to live up to the principles of life, liberty, and the pursuit of happiness to all within her borders. I really want you to understand why America is incapable of being what many so desperately desire her to be. This will take us sharing a very telling historical account that exposes an original concept and deeply held beliefs. We will take this up in the next chapter.

If America is the land of the free and of opportunity, then why are so many denied the freedom of enjoying the ability to have the same opportunities as others? Again, is it because there are two Americas? One for whites and the other for Black people? One for the rich and the other for the poor? If America is the land of plenty, then why do so many people have to subsist on mere morsels? Is this because you need the masses on the bottom to support your pyramidic system of governing?

Why does America boast the biggest prison population in the world? Why is the U.S. population only 5% of the world's population, yet have 25% of the worlds prisoners? What does this say about you America? What kind of nation are you really? Why is there this great disparity when compared to the rest of the world? You can tell a tree by the fruit it bears. And you can tell a lot about a government by the condition of its people. Can I pose a question? If I asked you, does slavery exist, in any form, in America, what would your answer be? Now, what if I told you that it does and that it can be easily proven? Well, let's let the record speak for itself by way of the thirteenth amendment to the Constitution of the United States.

Article XIII. [Thirteenth Amendment]
Prohibition of slavery
Section 1. *" Neither slavery nor involuntary servitude, except as a punishment for crime whereof the party have been duly convicted shall exist within the United States, or any place subject to their jurisdiction. "*

According to the language of this amendment, slavery is prohibited, unless you have been duly convicted of a crime. So, if you have been duly convicted of a crime, this allows you to be made a legal slave. Prisons are like modern day slave plantations, because everything about the prison experience parallels to the condition of slavery.
From the quality of the food. The clothing. The bedding. The wages. The treatment. The complete lack of human rights. You may say, well, prison is not supposed to be a vacation. People are there because they did something wrong. At the same time, the vast majority, upwards of 98% of everyone incarcerated, will one day return to society. Who do you want to return?
Criminologists, those who study crime and penal treatment, have uncovered what they consider as the root cause of crime. As I've said before, they don't penetrate deep enough into the primal cause because

the framework of American institutions are not designed to solve what they don't want solved. Suppose we take what you say to be accurate criminologist, what have you done with your findings? What actions were undertaken by you to help end or curb crime? What have you done to deal with social conditions that contribute to crime?

Fighting crime to you is focused primarily on arresting, imprisoning, and punishing those who break the law. Then you use harsh sentencing as a means to deter others from committing crimes. Don't you think that to really get up under crime, if that was your goal, that you would take your understanding of crime and tackle its causes? That way, crime would have no choice but to be greatly reduced. Otherwise it is like a doctor always treating the symptoms but never the disease itself. The pathology of crime, when left untreated, creates other problems in society.

It never ceases to amaze me why none of this is given the light of day when discussing crime and its prevention. If crime is so problematic, and it most definitely is, then wouldn't you want to canvass all possibilities that would lead to its elimination? If not, then this leads me to believe that there is something sinister involved when you have those in the know doing nothing to fix this problem.

To fix the crime problem would mean to interfere with a major aspect of a well-orchestrated scheme to trick and trap those who are less fortunate. It would mean to interfere with an industry that is a cash cow. Profits will always trump the lives of those seen as worthless.

I suppose you want the people to believe that with all of your smarts, resources, and capabilities that you can't get a handle on crime? We can't be that gullible to think that this problem is unsolvable. And this is why the term, 'the real profiteers of crime', was used in the previous chapter. Those labeled as undesirables of society are used to fuel this massive slave enterprise called the Prison Industrial Complex. The real objective is the mass enslavement of blacks which serves so many other purposes with one fell swoop.

The damaging effects that this has had on the black family is immeasurable. This then becomes the cause of many of the other problems that black people experience. When the man is absent, it is like taking one of the most effective pieces off the chessboard. No man present means there is no protector, no provider, no guider, and no one to set the example for the children of what it means to be a man, a husband, and a father. It creates a void that is filled in unnatural and costly ways.

Mass incarceration is an act of genocide. This makes it a weapon of mass destruction. The less informed might see this as an extreme proposition. The more informed already understand that one way to slow the birth rate of blacks as a means to counter the projection made by demographers of a black and brown majority in America in a matter of a decades is to lock black and brown people up wholesale. When it comes to the treatment of the incarcerated, how do you want those who are in prison to return to society? Better off or worse off? Even if you don't care how someone is treated who has been convicted of a crime, of which I can see the aversion; but you should be concerned how society could be impacted.

You don't think of the residual effects do you? Or you do, but these residual effects also serve your unjust ends? The bottom line is this, prisoners are legal slaves and are subject to a slave existence. I should not have to ask you what the effects of slavery are? But I will in the context of how many correctional officers have taken on the dual role of slave maker and slave overseer. While the wardens are themselves, the slave masters.

Chippewa Correctional Facility, where I'm currently housed, has an ominous acronym that describes it to perfection. URF, on paper stands for Upper Regional Facility. The unwritten other accepted meaning that it is known by, because of its Gestapo-like tactics and practices, is, You Are F#@*ed (U.R.F.). The level of injustice and arbitrary treatment that we are subjected to at this prison is, it seems, licensed and sanctioned by the Director of the MDOC. This is a disciplinary prison. That basis is used to strip you of every right imaginable. You are literally treated like a piece of fecal matter or dung.

There is little recourse that can be pursued that will remedy any legitimate grievance that you have other than to file a 42 U.S.C. 1983 civil rights suit. These civil complaints in prison have high hurdles to overcome to state a constitutional claim. Aside from your primary focus of going home, I would urge anyone doing time to become versed in their constitutional rights and prison policies and hold prison officials accountable when your rights are violated.

Everyone, administratively, from the top to the bottom, sees us as inhuman. And as such, we are treated less than human. This can cause us to take our frustrations out on one another, which plays right into their hands to further justify their barbaric treatment. Even when things escalate and violence reaches their doorstep, it is quickly quelled and normalcy resumes.

Prisons like URF has a practice of attempting to create a culture of fear as a means of control. But when you are fearless and know how to think, then you become a stumbling block and pose the greatest threat, which then makes you a special target When you are abusive and unjust for no reason other than to exact punishment, what do you think you will produce in others? Again, these are the same people that will one day return to society. Do you think your treatment will have a positive or a negative effect?

What do you have to say about this criminologists? Again, what do you do with your findings once you arrive at them? Or do you know this already but it is not in the interests of white supremacy to make the system more just, equitable, or fair?

Although crime and punishment go hand in hand, if you want to live in the dark ages and exact draconian style measures on prisoners, then that is your prerogative.

Do you know what you are doing when you do this? You are producing a more hardened and dangerous individual who will become more of a menace to society than they were before they got locked up. This could be why black people are more scrutinized and racially profiled by police in more affluent neighborhoods. And why there seems to be a better response time from police in those same neighborhoods. You have good reason to be afraid.

Is gentrification one of your other measures you have taken to keep the poor and disenfranchised away from where you live or want to live? All of this because you are well aware of what you have produced. The Blackman who acts like a savage with no sense is your handiwork. How can you condemn a product of your own creation?

I'm only bringing light to some of the things that go on in here because prison is the land of the forgotten. And it strips you not only of your freedom, but if you let it, it will strip you of your pride, dignity, and humanity. It can turn you into something that will even frighten you. You have to fight everyday just to maintain your sanity. At all costs, keep your manhood intact. They may not like you, but they will give you a certain deference if your presence commands it.

This does not mean they can't stand you, it only means they are careful how they deal with you. It is up to you to stay above the fray. They will wait for you to do something that will justify dealing with you a certain way. Do you mind if we go back to the term, 'duly convicted' in the aforementioned constitutional amendment? What does it mean to be duly convicted? Duly essentially means properly. Properly is something done thoroughly or completely. It also means being done correctly. But correctly from whose standpoint?

Now, if any of the premises laid out in this book are remotely close to being true, then how can any black person be duly convicted in America if her institutions are systemically racist? How can any black person be duly convicted if conditions were purposefully manufactured to facilitate the likelihood of committing a crime?

Not only do I take personal umbrage to that particular phraseology of being 'duly convicted', and its legitimacy in the broadest sense, but I think black people should be cleared of all charges and the slate wiped clean. Me saying this will have the same impact and effect of someone trying to blot out the light of the sun or trying to drain the oceans of its waters. But unless and until the playing field is leveled, then the rules and laws that you hold others to will only continue to contribute to the disproportionality of blacks being the burden bearers of an unjust criminal justice system because these laws will work against one person more than another. There is nothing 'duly' about that.

The 13th Amendment is inhumane and a massive breach of morality and reveals not only the purpose and intent of those who framed and constructed the language of this amendment, but it reveals the modern purpose and intent of today's politicians, lawmakers, and penologists who revert to this document's wording to justify their own wickedness. Prison - (Confinement); Industrial - (Forced Labor); Complex - (Mass

Warehousing). The Prison Industrial Complex is a place where people are housed, without the ability to leave, for the sole purpose of forced labor as a result of being convicted of a crime, unduly I might add. When I say forced labor that is exactly what I mean. You will be punished for not working, for literal slave wages.

Jobs that pay by the hour or by the day are laughable. You begin at .17 and half cents an hour. Or a job that pays you .84¢ a day. Combine this with the ever-increasing commissary prices and the dwindling quality of food served. Families, that are already poor to begin with are further drained of what little finances they have sending monies into the facility not wanting their incarcerated family members to go without basic necessities. This, as it drains the pockets of the poor, it handsomely fattens the pockets of those companies connected with or who are contracted to do business with the Prison Industrial Complex. Crime and big business go hand in hand.

This collateral damage to black families is another layer of suffering and deprivation that keeps the cycles of poverty, crime, imprisonment, teenage pregnancy, drug use, and family dysfunction going. If you are really concerned about improving society and making it safe and better for everyone, then you have the opportunity to do so by bringing as many resources to the table and using whatever expertise you need as you do with every other national emergency. The victims of a crime are not being discounted or disregarded. Neither is more sympathy being elicited for the families of a convicted felon over the families of those who were victimized. It goes without saying that the devastation that people and their families go through from being victimized is profound and life changing.

And just so the record is clear, there is never any valid reason, under any circumstances, to take money or property that does not belong to you. And there is definitely no excuse or justification to senselessly take someone else's life. Crime, even though it is a scourge to society, has always sadly been this sort of phenomenon with the public. And people, although they are not criminals, and have no desire to be one, they have this sordid fascination with crime, criminals, and crime stories.

Look at all of the movies, T.V. shows, and crime specials that deal with crime. If the ratings were not so high then some of these movies would not still be in rotation years after their release. Television shows wouldn't have franchised if the demand was not there. And crime specials would not be worth airing. You call it art imitating life, but they are really fictional portrayals of reality that is life in art form that allows people to experience the culture of crime and the criminal life vicariously through these storylines and different characterizations.

Even real crime specials are of great interest to the public. I don't know the psychology of why this is, but the attraction is there. I know that no one wants to either commit a crime or be the victim of one, but through the safety of TV, it makes it okay and gives people a front-row seat without having to actually be there or be a part of it.

Drug dealing has long been sensationalized and glamorized through movies like Scarface, Blow, and American Gangster. I know these movies have an indelible influence over black youth who aspire to have money that will give them a lifestyle that they think only drug dealing can bring. So they are drawn into the gravitational pull of what that lifestyle can offer them. What did you think would happen when you dangled that carrot in front of the eyes of those who are starving to get out of poverty? Especially when they are cut off from many other viable ways to make big money?

You knew exactly what would happen. Your scheme worked. And you profited both ways. First, at the box office; and secondly, in the new cadre of young black drug dealers these movies inspired to a life of crime. A life of crime that would eventually end in death or prison. Let's move on to the matter of rehabilitation as we close. This term is incongruent with prison because you won't be rehabilitated unless you take it upon yourself to divest yourself of a certain way of thinking and certain actions that caused you to end up in prison in the first place.

The rehabilitation or reformation process is one that involves deep introspection and coming out of that introspection with a resolve to never allow yourself to engage in crime again because you realize that a criminal is not who you are. Once you come into a higher understanding of who you are and what your purpose in life is, then you will see crime as too far beneath you to commit. And you will be ashamed of what you have allowed yourself to become. I know I am. And on top of the shame is the intense regret which is a burden that you may have to carry for the rest of your life.

At some point though, when you clean yourself up enough and make the necessary corrections, you must forgive yourself. And then you must learn to use your prior bad acts as a means to help you in becoming a more productive member of society and your community for yourself and your family. Rehabilitation means taking it upon yourself to become a better person. To restore your mental health. To become more concerned with the rights of others and vowing never to violate those rights. Once you make your mind up to do this, it is as good as done. You know better than anyone else how you think.

Don't let prison rob you of the potential to come out better than you went in. Don't let the inhumanity you experience in prison make you hard and callous, because it can harden your heart. Use that unpleasantness as a motivating factor to do better and to be a better version of yourself. With that, I want to end with a quote that reflects what real prison reform is.

"True prison reform starts with the enlightenment of the inmate of who that inmate is in reality and not what he or she has become because of circumstances. True prison reform connects the soul to its Creator and begins to provide those human needs and then we see a change in attitude in the inmate that leads to behavioral change." The Honorable Minister Louis Farrakhan

9_ The Weight of Injustice

I want to get right into a historical landmark legal case that will be the central theme of this chapter. It will give us an inside view of what the prevailing attitude of white people was when this case was ruled on in the United States Supreme Court and how that same attitude exists today. My purpose is to show you, from the words of a Supreme Court justice why black people have always been treated like second-class citizens. I want to show you, from the words of this justice, why justice for us has always been denied. You might think that there is no way people think like that today. Think again.

Remember, talking about race is one of the three most explosive and controversial subjects to talk about outside of politics and religion. When we look back at history and recount what happened, it is not easy to hear the brutal and callous nature of the truth of the words and actions that came from one people to another people. But if we want to fully understand the reality of what is, it cannot be done without fully understanding the reality of what was. You can't get around truth if you want clarity. You can't get around truth if you want solutions. You can't get around truth if you want peace. And you can't get around truth if you want justice.

Peace will never come if the justice that is its bedrock is not given. And if the truth is removed from the equation, then justice can't be had.

Yes, the truth hurts. And it is easier to try to move forward in a dreamy kind of way hoping that modern changes can magically fix what centuries of lying, murdering, lynching, enslavement, Jim Crow, and injustice has produced. But it can't.

When we introduced this book, we said that when blacks and whites are mentioned it is not referring to every single black person or every single white person. So, to the white people who are removed from the attitude of what will follow, you still know there are white people who think what I'm about to highlight. Some white folks feel as if they have an exclusive birthright to the inalienable rights bestowed upon them by their Creator as if the same Creator didn't bestow upon black people those same inalienable rights. When you read in the Preamble to the Constitution of the United States that they will, 'secure the blessings of liberty for themselves and their posterity...', that is a creed they live by. What does posterity mean? It means offspring. It also means all future generations.

We are not the offspring of white people, so the blessings of liberty didn't include us. This attitude was embodied in Donald Trump's mantra of 'Make America Great Again'. Why do you think MAGA was so popular? Why do you think it struck such a powerful cord in a lot of white people? That theme was a hit. Donald Trump is idolized by his base as their saving grace because he was unafraid to be a voice and catalyst to secure those blessings of liberty to the posterity of white people.

That mantra contained a hidden message to those class of whites who have always felt that black people were destined to be hewers of wood, drawers of water, and the burden bearers of society. We were never to be afforded the same rights as whites. The United States Supreme Court case of Dred Scott v. Sandford, in 1857, underscores why knowing history is so important. Understanding the past gives you a better understanding of the present. But when we don't know the history of the past, we are left blind to just how deep the race problem really is.

Let's get into it. Read the below words and we will comment intermittently:

"The judgment finding that respondent was not liable to petitioner for assault was reversed and the case was remanded with an order to dismiss the action for lack of jurisdiction. The Supreme Court held that petitioner was not a citizen and could not bring the action in the court because petitioner was a slave of African descent...".

"The court held that petitioner was a slave and, therefore, petitioner was merely property and respondent was allowed to treat his property as he thought appropriate...".

"The court held that petitioner was not a citizen of Missouri...as asserted in his original complaint because he was not permitted to become a citizen, and no state had the power to grant him citizenship...".

A black person was never considered a citizen, nor could a black person ever be made a citizen. Later on in these quotes you will see that this was a perpetual position by the founding fathers that they never wanted any deviation from. That they did this with a sound mind and clear intention.

"... And for this reason it(any state) cannot introduce any person, or description of persons, who were not intended to be embraced in this neo political family, which the Constitution brought into existence, but were intended to be excluded from...".

"The words 'people of the United States' and 'citizen' are synonymous terms, and mean the same thing. They both describe the political body who, according to republican institutions, form the sovereignty, and who hold the power and conduct the Government through their representatives. They are what the court familiarly calls sovereign people, and every citizen is one of this people, and a constituent member of the sovereignty...".

Since blacks are excluded from citizenship, and the word 'citizen' is synonymous with the words, 'we the people', it stands true that the constitution was made of white people, for white people, and by white people. And Donald Trump only lived up to the oath he took to preserve,

TERRY TRIGGS

protect, and defend the Constitution of the United States by protecting the rights of whites.

"Every person, and every class and description of persons, who were at the time of the adoption of the Constitution recognized as citizens in the several states, became also citizens of this new political body, but none other; it was formed by them, and for them and their posterity, but for no one else...".

"The word 'citizen' in the Constitution does not embrace one of the negro race --- negro cannot become a citizen --- Declaration of Independence does not include slaves as part of the people... the rights and privileges conferred by the Constitution upon citizens do not apply to the negro race...".

"The provisions of the Constitution of the United States in relation to the personal rights and privileges to which the citizen of a state should be entitled, do not embrace the negro African race, at that time in this country, or who might afterwards be imported, who had then been or should afterwards be made free in any state...".

"The language in the Declaration of Independence, show that neither the class of persons who had been imported as slaves, nor their descendants, whether they had become free or not, were then

acknowledged as part of the people, nor intended to be included in the general words used in the instrument...".

"The descendants of Africans who were imported into this country and sold as slaves, when they shall become emancipated, or who are born of parents who had become free before their birth, are not citizens of a state in the sense in which the word 'citizen' is used in the Constitution of the United States...".

"The enslaved African race was not to be included in, and formed no part of, the people who framed and adopted the Declaration of Independence...".

I don't want to bore you with these apparent redundancies, however, each of these quotes has distinct elements that I don't want us to be without the knowledge of. We are almost there though. These words are a searing reminder to all those who believe that times have changed in regards to certain rights and privileges being for everyone. Remember when we spoke about white privilege in chapter two, the constitution codified the privilege of whites. And systems were established to ensure its staying power. A few more quotes, so bear with me.

"When the framers of the Constitution were conferring special rights and privileges upon citizens of a state in every other part of the Union, it

TERRY TRIGGS

is possible to believe that these rights and privileges were intended to be extended to the negro race...".

"A state may afford you a right or a privilege, but that will not make him a citizen of the United States...".

"The change in public opinion and feeling in relation to the African race, which has taken place since the adoption of the Constitution, cannot change its construction and meaning, and it must be construed and administered now according to its true meaning and intention when it was formed and adopted more than a century ago regarded the negro as an inferior, and unfit to associate with the white race, socially and politically... so far inferior, that they had no rights which the white man was bound to respect; and that the negro might justly and lawfully be reduced to slavery for his benefit...".

No matter how much attitudes have changed in some, these changing attitudes cannot change the construction and meaning of the constitution or declaration of independence and it must be construed or interpreted according to its true intention and purpose. What was its intent an purpose? To make black people perpetual slaves. These are powerful words that should shock your conscience and make you cringe. Blacks never had any rights that white people were bound to respect.
And lastly, to drive the point home even further;

"The men who framed the declaration were great men...high in literary acquirements...they knew that no one in the civilized world would embrace the negro race, which, by common consent, had been excluded from civilized Governments and the family of nations, and doomed to slavery...".

The entire white world was in agreement to keep black people blocked from being recognized as a civilized nation or government. Just look at how African nations are seen and dealt with today by white nations. This same sentiment is still at play. I know that this was extensive, but I wanted to give you as much of the meat of the idea as was necessary to make this argument crystal clear of why we have never received the justice that we have been fighting for. The idea of white rule must be preserved at all costs.

The progress that we have made up to this point is not because of the benevolence of white people. No! We have fought for every right we have secured for ourselves. And we still have such a long way to go. How many other jurists do you think have these same view points and interpretations of the constitution? What about those in the U.S. Senate and House of Representatives? Don't you think they are well versed in the language of the constitution? Do they see its 'true meaning and intention' as did the judge who ruled in Dred Scott v. Sandford in 1857? Could this be the reason why there was so much resistance to the right for equal education as in Brown v. Board of Education? Or the right to vote as fought for in the voting rights act? When are we going to realize that it is the government, the rulers, who determine how justice is meted out. Not the little guy?

Black people were brought to America for one reason, and one reason only, to be made slaves for whites. Did we come of our own free-will? Or by brute force, subterfuge, and trickery? We ended up in chains in the holds of ships crammed in like sardines. We had to relieve ourselves on ourselves. We were not seen as human beings, but as merchandise to profit from. The slave trade was big business. This history can't be swept under the rug as if it didn't happen. The effects of that history still lives on today.

What we have been through does not define us. Yet, what we have been through has shaped us and made us into a something that is miles apart from what God made. This is the effect of centuries of slavery and injustice. It has been a weight that we have had to carry for centuries. The emancipation proclamation only ended chattel slavery, but it did not sever the cord of control of white people over black lives. We are only partially free. We won't experience a full and complete freedom until the umbilical cord is cut.

All we know is America. Even with all her evils, America is still the greatest nation on earth. And yes there is plenty of opportunity to excel here more than anywhere else. That still does not take away from institutionalized racism that makes black people have to work twice as hard just to get ahead.

Patriotism is good. You should have national pride and love for your country. This does not mean that everything about your nation or country is good or right. There are many nations on the earth whose form of rulership is tyrannical and the people they rule over suffer because of it.

America rules very similarly as other despots. The only difference is she wears a velvet glove. This makes her tyranny soft to the touch or less outwardly abrasive. She uses more finesse.

I remember in elementary school reciting the 'pledge of allegiance' every morning. There I stood with my right hand over my heart, being inculcated to love a country that hated me. That was the hand rocking the cradle. I was being psychologically influenced subtly. I didn't know what a pledge was. I didn't know what allegiance meant either. Yet, I pledged allegiance to the flag of the United States and to a Republic for which I knew not what it stood for.

A flag that I suffered under and did not see me as an equal. A Republic that stood for a power that subjugated blacks and only secured the rights of whites. This is what I was pledging my allegiance to. The words in the preamble to the United States Constitution, the Declaration of Independence, and the Pledge of Allegiance are a perfect idea of a perfect world. But America is far from perfect and true justice is still not given to all who live under the stars and stripes.

This book would not be written if those ideals were a reality for blacks in America. They are not. Justice is not for all, but for the privileged few. It is for the rich and for those who have friends in high enough places to circumvent justice. Justice is one of the constant themes mentioned in all three of the above early documents of the United States. So what is justice?

Justice is fair dealing. It is supposed to be blind and applied equally to all. But in America, justice is far from fair and it is far from blind. Justice has been for those who can pay for it or those who are lucky enough to slip through the cracks. Injustice is like a boomerang, it is something that will one day return to its sender. Whether you are an individual or a nation, we all reap what we sow.

Reaping can be immediate, intermediate, or much later. But you can't escape it. Wrongdoing never prospers. The pendulum of justice is always at work and injustice won't be able to find refuge from it. Continued injustice has America on a collision course with her demise. And if she doesn't right her wrongs, injustice will be the means by which her end is met.

Human nature demands justice. And when you deprive a human being of something it needs to function properly, you produce an imbalance in the individual. This imbalance occurs in the mind. And just like with anything that is not balanced, it is unable to sustain itself for very long. Whether you are black or white, if you don't like what is going on when it comes to blacks speaking out or acting out in response to injustice, then do something about it. What do I mean by do something about it? Use your voice and platform to speak out against injustice and advocate for systemic changes.

If you won't help solve what is going on between the races, then what right do you have to complain about how people feel and how they react to what is being done to them? From where I stand, you don't have a right to interject an opinion in the matter if you choose to stay on the sidelines while this drama is playing out. Let those out there fighting for their life fight the best way they know how and in whatever manner they choose to.

You don't know what the weight of injustice feels like. It is a crushing weight. The mind can only handle so much. And when you couple injustice with other factors, things can get overwhelming. Things have been simmering for a while now. The boil is on the horizon. Injustice is also a contributing factor in many of the mental health problems that black people suffer from. This leads to other problems. When you deal with something in isolation, you sometimes fail to see how one condition is connected to a broader condition.

The way this world is set up and operates, these effects are foreseen well in advance by the wise who know how our natures will respond when you don't feed it what it needs. We just said that human nature demands justice. And we already showed what happens when that demand is not met. What happens when your body is deficient of a vitamin, mineral, or some other nutrient? Does this effect your health in any way? Can a single deficiency in one area of the body lead to other health complications in other areas of the body?

Once a doctor discovers what's missing, he knows exactly what to prescribe to nurse the body back to health. Your body needs a balanced diet in order to stay healthy. The health of the mind is no different. When human needs are not met, the health of the mind is at risk. What are those needs?

What I'm about to share now is generally known by all of us in one way or another, but it does no hurt to remind us sometimes of what we already know. Besides, it fits the context of this chapter. The needs are knowledge, wisdom, and understanding; freedom, justice, and equality; food, clothing, and shelter; and love, peace, and happiness. These are the main ingredients needed for the human mind and spirit to be balanced and healthy. Each of these needs can be elaborated on to explain how they are all interrelated. However, at present our focus is on the weight of injustice.

If a dietician can put together a menu that contains the proper nutritional needs to maintain the health of the body, then why can't it be done by mental healthcare professionals to maintain the health of the mind? The powers that be know what these human needs are, how to provide these human needs, and what the effects are when these human needs are not met. You should never expect the perpetrators of injustice to be your saving grace. Instead, produce and supply these needs yourself? Why wait for someone else to give you what you can give yourself?

But as long as you, or any of us, who are without these needs, remain blind, deaf, and dumb and sit around and wait for someone else, then our condition will remain unchanged. We have to stop acting like we are handicapped. Blindness here is having eyes but not being able to recognize or understand what you are looking at. Deafness is having ears but you find it difficult to hear and accept the truth. Dumb does not mean stupid. It means your inability to speak clearly and with wisdom because you have accepted the lie as the truth and the truth as a lie.

Above all, we have to stop being unjust to ourselves and others. Injustice, no matter where it comes from, has the same effect. We can't continue to treat each other the way we have been. There is no excuse for us to mistreat one another the way we do. We have to stop being agents in our own destruction. Look at our condition, we are in a state of disarray and dysfunction. Some of us literally can't stand the sight of each other? How is that possible? Where did something like that come from? There is nothing normal about that. We are sick and we need a prescription to help restore us. Justice, along with the other mentioned needs is just what the doctor ordered.

We have been turned upside down and inside out and have become so hateful of each other. We don't have to look no further than our own family dynamic. I know it's crazy and it makes no sense. But this is what you get when you deprive human beings of basic human rights. People are literally driven to insanity and they don't know why. It is hard to rationalize the truth of how things got this way so we choose to escape by whatever means that will give us just a piece of peace so we don't have to face reality.

I want to make this last statement as we end this chapter. I have been sentenced to die in your prison for aiding abetting a robbery. Your system has fashioned it so that a person's role in the crime of robbery that unfortunately leads to the loss of life, even if they lack the requisite intent to kill, is guilty of murder. How unjust is that? This is the law in Michigan. But, just because there is a law that determines what constitutes culpability, does not make that law right or fair? Again, you have to go back to how, who, when, and for what purpose was this law constructed.

Once you realize something can be improved and made better, then you need to take the necessary steps to make those improvements. The state of California recognized this and made revisions to their felony murder law that reflects justice. Why can't Michigan do the same? I have a legitimate right to my position, because in my opinion, the ends of justice was not served. You may not like what is being said or how it is being said, and perhaps it could be said differently, but I'm not a politician. Therefore, I am not bound by the same rules of that game that makes people bow down and genuflect even when they know what they are bowing to is wrong.

I will never compromise my personal integrity to appease you. Yes, my present condition is the result of my own unjust actions. So, I am very well acquainted with the effects of how being unjust in your actions can cause a very regrettable consequence. This book is a product of not only your injustice, but of my own.

10_ By Any Means Necessary

In my opinion, black people have always been seen by white elitists as a stain to be blotted out. This blotting was to be done, and is being done, by any means necessary. What we want to do here is dig a little deeper into the sophisticated, comprehensive, and innovative ways the elites are achieving their objectives.

Our aim is to tie all of the loose strands of this book together to give us a more concrete understanding of a very specific coordinated stealthy attack against black, brown, and other so-called minorities. It is important to remember that the perspective of the one who is oppressed will always be different from the one who oppresses. The two will never see oppression the same way.

The oppressed, aside from social media, doesn't have access to the same major media platforms as the oppressor. The oppressor's narratives are able to be constantly aired through major news outlets. The sheer force of repetition, even if its misinformation, is enough produce a slight psychological edge in the war of information. What do I mean by that? When you can provide the material that forms the basis of the thinking of the people, then invariably, the people will begin to think like you.

This explains why there is so much resistance and outright rejection of the truth when it is presented. It's because the masses have been trained to fight against their own liberation by denying the truth of the reality of what should be by accepting the false reality of what is.

This creates a very tricky proposition because one must be concerned with the manner of how they share valuable information. The truth teller must use tact in order to be more effective in getting over to the people a message that will help lift them out of their condition.

There is a verse in the Bible that I would like to use to describe the main point I want to make. That verse will shed light on what this writer means when he says, 'By Any Means Necessary'.

I will do this by using an exegetical argument. And exegetical argument is an explanation or critical interpretation of a text. The condition of the people is such that it needs to be explained from a biblical perspective. If our present condition can't be found in scripture, then we are lost beyond measure.

I'm not a scriptural scientist by any stretch of the imagination. The only religion I ever knew about or was acquainted with growing up was Christianity. I was not a devout practitioner of that faith by any means. Christianity was my family's faith of choice through tradition.

That background became the backdrop of my religious ideology. It served to acquaint me with many of the stories of the Bible from a general standpoint. I never thought to look beneath the surface or behind those stories to consider any hidden, deeper, or esoteric meanings.

My mind was always focused on the story itself. I had no reason to venture beyond what and how I was being taught. Little did I know, my acceptance of those stories on face value alone would put me in a time

133

warp which prevented me from grasping any transcendental meanings or deep treasures of wisdom buried in those stories. It is written that one should, 'Get wisdom, it is the principle thing, but with all thy getting, get understanding.'.

The wisdom that could be obtained from the Bible was made void to me because I did not have a firm understanding of the lessons many of those biblical stories contained. I never once considered correlating the past with the present until a stranger knocked on the door of my mind with a couple of thought-provoking questions.

I was asked, "Where are you in the Bible?". "Where are black people in the Bible?". And, "Where is America in the Bible?".
I could not answer any of those questions. But it did make me think. I thought about traditional history books that only spoke of past persons or events. I saw the Bible as a history book. But since God was part of the equation, I rationalized that the Bible could not be an ordinary history book about the past without it having a direct bearing on the present. Otherwise it would lose some of its relevance.

My mind, being stretched by those questions, made me open to the possibility of something more. If the Bible only contained stories of yesterday without any bearing on today, then why put so much stock in it I thought? I told you I saw religion as a chief tool in controlling the masses. In the past, Black people were locked out of the Bible, so why all of a sudden are we going to be given a true interpretation of the Bible? How could we get the true interpretation of the Bible by someone

who enslaved us, or by those who beat, killed, and maimed us?
That said, in the book of Exodus, it reads

, *"Come on, let us deal wisely with them, lest they multiply, and it come to pass, that, when there falleth out any war, they join also unto our enemies, and fight against us, and so get them up out of the land."*.
Exodus 1:10 KJV

I think if we parse that verse we will find many parallels to today. The invitation in the above passage by wise likeminded rulers and high government officials forms a secret plot and alliance to deal with black people, not foolishly, but very craftily. When you use wisdom, you are able to exercise a high degree of mastery to control circumstances, events, and conditions.

What does it mean when demographers predict a future when blacks and browns will be the majority if birth rates between blacks, browns, and whites remain consistent? It means that you have a reason to plot and plan. That fact alone provides motive. It also explains why someone would go to extreme lengths to destroy another people if they think they could lose their position. It explains why someone would use any men as necessary.

If one people's birthrate is on the rise, Blacks and Hispanics; and another's is on the decline, Whites; then drastic measures must be taken so that Whites are not supplanted by a growing minority birthrate. If this means employing every trick of the trade in their arsenal, no matter how wicked, and no matter how low down, dirty or underhanded, then so be it. The ends will justify their means.

What other reason would one people have to join on with another people unless they think one day those that they oppressed will learn that they have a common enemy that is the root cause of their condition? This is why the tactic to divide and conquer has been so useful against us. Any voice that is able to unite a divided people is considered dangerous and an enemy by those whose rule and control is made more effective if the people remain disunited and at odds with each other.

All means will be used to demonize the friend of the poor and disenfranchised. When you think about it, who speaks for the poor? Who speaks for the little person? When the poor respond, like soldiers, to a commander's voice, a voice of wisdom and guidance, then that is a voice that must be silenced, by any means necessary.

Although we have a handful of strong leaders, I can't think of any other voice that speaks to our condition more insightfully and more forcefully than The Honorable Minister Louis Farrakhan. His fearless stance, faithful service, and wise guidance is something that makes him like an oasis in a desert for many black people. But he is hated by the government. And for some strange reason, we are not allowed to show our love and support for him in any way. Why? What has he done other than be a champion for the little people? What crime has he committed? You don't like what he has to say, why? What can you point to that makes him unworthy of our support?

Some black people don't like The Minister and they don't even know him. What makes you not like him? What did he do to you? Is it because of what he teaches? How he teaches? What's wrong with you? You don't like the medicine called truth? We should not let shallow things divide us against each other. And we should not let anyone tell us who we can and cannot love and support.

We can't afford to let theological, ideological, or philosophical differences put a wedge between us. God is not divisive nor is He the author of confusion. But His truth exposes and separates the real ones from the pretenders. So who or what has you so confused? Do you think it is of your own doing? Or do you think you have adopted the view of the leaders of this world as your own when it comes to him? Be honest.

This reminds me of the Willie Lynch letter to slave owners in 1712. We must like or dislike who we are told to like or dislike. We must love or hate who we are told to love or hate. Our faith and trust must never be in one of our own. We were taught to love, fear, and trust only you. This is a sickness tied to weakness, fear, and an inferiority complex. I only bring The Minister up in this way at this juncture because no one has shed more light on or tackled the race issue the way he has. His words are always powerful, direct, and clear.

Let's get back to these wise dealings. I read a book that said that you can't catch a bird with one square of a net if you only used one square. But if you used a whole net, only one square in that net is needed to catch a bird. A net has been cast, far and wide.

There is not one single trap that has been laid before us. If that was the case, we could sidestep it. But a series of traps have been strategically set. And one of them, working together with the others, will be able to accomplish its goal. And all of them collectively, will get many of us.

These are the systems mentioned in this book. This is the unwritten Jim Crow laws. This is the war on drugs and the war on poverty. This is the predatory lending practices. This is inferior education. Bad healthcare. Poor quality food. The criminal justice system. Everything must be done to 'get them out the land'. Our people are dying and suffering. And the way it is being done is so wickedly masterful.

What has us looking like men on the outside, but the thinking, the faculty of reasoning, and the desire to be productive is absent on the inside? What has poisoned us like this? What wise tactics have been employed to make us our own worst enemies? Why are we the number one killers of ourselves? How did we become so divided as a people? I am saying that we have be dealt with wisely because there is a real fear of what our unity can do for us and them.

Black people, it is good that we are up in arms about police brutality and the killing of unarmed black men and women. But what about all of this black on black violence? When is the same outrage that we have when a police officer unjustifiably kills us but we are mostly silent when we kill us? What's that all about? What made us where we can snuff out our own lives without conscience?

I want to repeat this, we are not natural enemies of one another. I don't care how much in disagreement we become with each other, it should never lead to violence. We have to learn how to handle our disagreements on the basis of truth, justice, and what is right.

'Let us deal wisely with them...'. Cars, cellphones, and computers have underwent innovative changes to keep current with modern society.

The ability to take the same product and revolutionize it year after year to keep it relevant and more efficient takes creativity and innovation. If a certain prevailing attitude exists by whites that thinks black people should be perpetual slaves, then in order to accomplish that in this day and time, there needs to be a more advanced and sophisticated approach to keep people mentally and psychologically enslaved. That is not the workings of a fool but of someone who uses wisdom wickedly.

This, in my opinion, is what we have been up against.

This scripture is a modern up to date picture of what we are being confronted with. Why do you think the American Dream is more of a mirage that is something, if you achieve it, is meant to placate and pacify you? It is meant to give you an illusion of making it. It also serves to silence you to the larger issues of society and the world because you have no way of relating to the struggle. And you don't want to do anything to awaken from your dream or have it somehow taken from you.

Look at the language, American Dream. What is the American Dream? Is it having a middle class job, living in the suburbs with your wife and children, and being able to enjoy a life free from the injustices experienced by the poor? Is it having a 401k or IRA so you can have a comfortable retirement? Sadly and unfortunately, whatever the American Dream is, millions of Americans will never realize it. Even if it does consist of the above, those are only crumbs.

Haven't you been warned in the Bible not to be satisfied with crumbs that fall from the master's table? What is a crumb? It is an unintentional infinitesimally small piece of bread that is a natural result from biting a sandwich. You mean to tell me this is what you are so happy over? An unintentional benefit? You didn't know that the system is designed for a certain percentage of people to fit within the American Dream sphere? Do you know what a dream is? It is having or experiencing a series of thoughts, images, feelings, or emotions during sleep.

Sleep is a suspended state of consciousness. The closest many of us will ever get to the American Dream is on our sleep. The American Dream is a fantasy like life that keeps you in a suspended state of consciousness where you are not able to perceive reality correctly because you are asleep. The American Dream keeps you unconscious and blinded to reality because you are caught up in the rapture that is the American Dream.

You don't think you can do more or achieve more unless you get a middle class job working for someone else and not for yourself? And you feed this to your children. Go to school. Get a good job. And be satisfied. This reminds me of children born in slavery never knowing they were slaves until they were told they were because that is all they ever knew. What if I told you that you are a slave and don't even know it? You are a slave to the powers that be and you don't even know it. And you are trained to get along so you don't get whatever you have taken from you.

You know you are a slave when you are told who you can accept as your leader. And don't you dare choose someone or throw your support behind someone that does not have our stamp of approval. If you do you will be quickly reminded who the boss is. Their power of control over our lives is flexed whenever they feel it is necessary to remind us that we are still slaves, and they are still our masters.

Even if you are rich, you still have to play ball. It has happened too many times and it is played out on the world stage for all to see. This puts other black people on notice to tow the line. If not, this is what will happen to you too. So, what is the solution to many of the problems that we face on a daily basis? Is there a single solution that will fix all of our problems? Or does each problem warrant its own unique response?

I will repeat what is widely understood as the main ingredient that we can use to fix the majority of what we suffer from almost instantly. I will then share what is perhaps a seemingly more drastic solution no matter how unrealistic it looks on the surface.

First of all, unity is the key. It is the only way we can accomplish things that seem insurmountable. We will always be limited, picked off, or not as effective when we try to do things individually and on our own. This will involve having to subordinate our egos for the sake of advancement. Do you think you can do that for the greater good?

It is vanity to want to be seen and known as the main man even if it costs us a better future. It shouldn't matter who is out front or riding point as long as we move closer to true freedom and real justice. If one benefits we all benefit. The reward for this small sacrifice is a better life for us and our children. Now, what usually happens in a marriage when you have a husband and a wife with marital problems? Is their first option divorce? Or is it some form of counseling to try to resolve any disputes so that the marriage can be saved?

You would think that both parties would want to sit down and have the problems in the marriage ironed out by honestly and clearly putting their problems on the table to see if there is a way to reconcile things so they can go forward in a better way. What if talking is not enough? What if the same problems keep happening again and again and again? How long before you say hold on now, enough is enough.

What am I saying? I'm saying, that even though God does not like divorce, under certain circumstances He permits divorce as a remedy to maintain peace and balance.

What is the number one documented reason a divorcing party cites as to why they are filing for divorce? Irreconcilable differences. When two people find it impossible to live with in peace together, then, as a last resort, divorce or separation may be the best and only option. Before you think separation to be an absurdity, please read the Declaration of Independence in the next chapter.

We have to explore every possible solution available if it will end our suffering. How miserable would life be to live with someone who you simply can't get along with in peace? Ask any divorced person why they couldn't stay in the marriage any longer. Aside from infidelity, I wonder what they would say. Divorce for them was a relief. Like a weight had been lifted. These are just thoughts. But something has to be done, by any means necessary.

11_ A More Excellent Way

In this chapter we will examine the words of the founding fathers who were the architects and framers of the foundational principles and ideals that are supposed to be the bedrock of America. Measure these words and see for yourself if America is living up to these principles. If America has fallen short of what was so eloquently written during the inception of this nation, then according to what was written, what must be done? What can be done? And what should be done?

You will discover after carefully studying these words and examining them, that if these things were carried into practiced, it would be the kind of world and society that the American people long for. Also, compare these written principles and promises and compare them to what some of our leaders have been saying for years who have been on the front lines fighting for a piece of justice. The fight for real freedom and true justice has been something we have had to fight for centuries.

The institutions in America were established during the period of slavery, so were these documents. You have to ask yourself, were you included in what was written? Was the government really of, for, or by you? America has yet to evolve to be reflective of what her potential is. If she is to survive, she must.

These words also contain the keys to your rights. But there is no sense on having rights if you don't exercise them. America exists because she exercised her right to be free from the abuses she suffered at the hands of Great Britain. She fought against and separated herself from the cruelty and tyranny of a government who was unconcerned with the general welfare of its citizens.

America's strength lies in her moral uprightness and her adherence to the promise she made of life, liberty and the pursuit of happiness The people have the right, and the duty, to hold America accountable. The words that comprise these documents are perfect, yet the practice of them are not. What did the writers mean by the words, 'a more perfect union? How can you take something that is perfect and make it more perfect?

The principles of freedom and justice, and life and happiness, are not static principles, they must evolve as the nation evolves. If not, the death of that nation is inevitable. Any true patriot would realize that all human beings do have certain inalienable rights, and that it is not wrong to hold America's feet to the fire and make her responsible for and responsive to the needs of those who live within her boarders. This would seem to me to be the most American thing you could do. And this would seem to be, to me, a more excellent way.

* The Preamble to the Constitution of the United States
We the People of the United States, in Order to form a more perfect Union, establish Justice, insure domestic Tranquility, provide for the common defense, promote the general Welfare, and secure the Blessings

of Liberty to ourselves and our posterity, do ordain and establish this Constitution for the United States of America.

* Article I. [First Amendment]

Religious establishment prohibited. Freedom of speech and of press; right to assemble and to petition.

Congress shall make no law respecting an establishment of religion, or prohibiting the free exercise thereof; or abridging the freedom of speech, or of the press; or of the right of the people peaceably to assemble, and to petition the Government for a redress of grievances.

* The Declaration of Independence

When in the Course of human Events, it becomes necessary for one People to dissolve the Political Bands which have connected them with another, and to assume among the Powers of the Earth, the separate and equal Station to which the Laws of Nature and of Nature's God entitle them, a decent Respect to the Opinions of Mankind requires that they should declare the causes which impel them to the Separation.

We hold these Truths to be self-evident, that all Men are created equal, that they are endowed by their Creator with certain unalienable Rights, that among these are Life, Liberty, and the Pursuit of Happiness ---

That to secure these Rights, Governments are instituted among Men, deriving their just Powers from the Consent of the Governed, that whenever any Form of Government becomes destructive of these Ends, it is the Right of the People to alter or abolish it, and to institute new Government, laying its Foundation on such Principles, and organizing its Powers in such Form, as to them shall seem most likely to affect their Safety and Happiness.

Prudence, indeed, will dictate that Governments long established should not be changed for light and transient Causes; and accordingly all Experience hath shewn, that Mankind are more disposed to suffer, while Evils are sufferable, than to right themselves by abolishing the Forms to which they are accustomed.

But when a long Train of Abuses and Usurpations, pursuing invariably the same Object, evinces a Design to reduce them under absolute Despotism, it is their Right, it is their Duty, to throw off such Government, and to produce new Guards for their future Security. Such has been the patient Sufferance of these Colonies; and such is now the Necessity which constrains them to alter their former Systems of Government.

The History of the present King of Great-Britain is a History of repeated Injuries and Usurpations, all having in direct Object the Establishment of an absolute Tyranny over these States. To prove this, let Facts be submitted to a candid World.

* The Pledge of Allegiance

I pledge allegiance to the flag of the United States of America, and to the republic for which it stands, one nation under God, indivisible, with liberty and justice for all.

* Oath of Office

I do solemnly swear (or affirm) that I will faithfully execute the office of

President of the United States, and will to the best of my Ability, preserve, protect, and defend the Constitution of the United States. After reading these documents, it should be clear to you that America never had us in mind when any of these documents were written. When you understand this, the ruling by the Justice in the Dred Scott case makes more sense.

The Dred Scott case that was mentioned in Chapter 9 gives an inside look into the thinking, attitudes, and beliefs that still exist to this day. America's understanding of the true intent and purpose of the founding fathers' words drives her domestic and foreign policies against anyone who is non-European. This is what we need to realize. High government officials have always known and understood something about this country that we don't. We have blindly carried this illusion with us that we are American citizens and that we are entitled to the same rights as others.

Well, this may be true in God's eyes, but this has never been true in the eyes of the white establishment. Our three-fifths status has never changed. We have always been seen as and treated like second-class citizens. And so, as America struggles to form a more perfect union, she is met with opposition because there is a segment in government and in society who likes things the way they have always been, which is the way things were always designed and intended to be.

Then there are others who want to amend and modify yesterday's thinking because they are moved by higher ideals and human empathy and compassion. Do not underestimate how cold, callous, and calculatedly cunning this former group is when it comes to preserving their idea of what they believe the constitution stands for.

All of you students of history, you know how evil America has been. You know that there is a fight going on with the people on the bottom for justice, and another fight going on at the top to prevent that justice from happening.

The only difference between today and yesterday by those in power is that things today are done more so with a smile, a pat on the back, and false promises. Don't be fooled by this posturing. America has evolved her tactics to ensure that black people never receive real justice.

If I tell you I love you, but my actions tell you a different story, what are you going to believe more? My words or my actions? If my actions don't measure up to the words I say, then I don't really mean what I say. I'm only paying lip service.

Through the prolific use of the science of argumentation and selective wording, coded terms and concepts are introduced that contains hidden meanings and messages. This is how old ideas are kept alive and new ones are introduced. Has it ever occurred to you why there is so much politicization of issues that should have no room for debate? But these ultraconservative power players have shrewd ways of giving the appearance of advancement which are really moves to reverse any advancements made.

Just look at the recent attempts to reverse the 1965 Voting Rights Act under the guise of making elections less susceptible to fraud. What about police reform? Even in the face of overwhelming indisputable evidence of the need for police reform, it is being debated about. For what? How is this a political issue when it should be a human rights issue? The handwriting is on the wall and the message is clear.

But this is a new day. And a new generation is emerging that is more courageous and more conscious than previous generations. This is no knock on those who paid a price and paved the way for where we are now. There have always been mass movements in the past to combat social injustice and the fight for civil rights, but it has never been on this level or to the degree that it is today.

And not surprisingly, the bulk of this group is the younger generation. And it is not just black people in the streets. Every race and ethnic group is being represented as wanting an end to injustice and systemic racism. We all have a vested interest in what is going on. We are all effected by this turmoil in some way.

This is not an easy subject to talk about. It is uncomfortable. It is controversial. Uncomfortability may be what's needed. And controversy may be the friction needed to move us forward. There will always be lingering issues that surface from time to time if we don't tackle the race issue head on.

Even institutional changes will have little effect if we don't stop passing along to our children biases and prejudices against someone because of their creed, class, or color. I heard Megan McCain speaking on the talk show 'The View' about the misinformation being disseminated by the CDC about the covid vaccines and vaccinating people. The CDC's messaging was not as effective in getting people vaccinated as they had hoped it. She described the hesitancy of many Americans refusing to get vaccinated as being "complicated because of America's history.".

Complicated. Is that the most suitable word to describe the history in question? What particular part of America's history is she making reference to that is so complicated that it would cause such hesitancy? Or were her words a euphemistic way of sweeping over a dark past? It is not really that complicated if we were honest about the atrocities committed by the U.S. Government, both in the past and in the present. It is more than the Tuskegee experiment when blacks were given syphilis without their knowledge or consent for forty years, from 1932-1972 to study its effects. Or lacing blankets with smallpox and giving them to the Native Americans under the pretense of helping them stay warm in the winter.

If you can do that, what else are you capable of doing? What other acts don't we know about that parallel or even dwarf these biological attacks? How difficult would it be to target large segments of a specific population group through biological means if that was your aim?

Can specific genotypes be targeted where one person with a specific genotype is more susceptible to a biological attack than those of another genotype if they take the same vaccine or medicine? So, she is right, the history of America is complicated to talk about because it would reveal things that would make you squirm in your seat by the mere thought of it. How would explain your wicked deeds? You know good and well that you have a past that you wish could be swept under the rug where it never sees the light of day.

Calling America's history 'complicated' is a misnomer and is beyond euphemistic. This kind of talk does nothing to help the problem and only further complicates matters. Why not uncomplicate things by explaining the history. Someone needs to tell the robe less emperor that he is naked. If straight words were spoken more regularly it would help make things less uneasy over time. The initial shock or abrasiveness of being direct, open, and honest will wear off and won't be as bad the more it happens. And soon the people will become acclimated to transparent truthful dialogue even if it is painful in the beginning.

You may say that it is not necessary to bring up every single thing that has happened in the past. That today we should be focusing on what the solutions are. I think you are right. Sometimes focusing on the positive will take care of the negative.

My argument would also be that knowing and understanding what happened in the past will help to formulate and come up with solutions that root out what was to prevent it from ever happening again.

You wouldn't go to a doctor's office and ask for a partial assessment of the condition of your health after you have been examined. No. You want and need to know the full extent of what is wrong with you health wise so that an accurate diagnosis can be made. Without the full truth of your medical condition, it won't allow a competent doctor to properly prescribe the right medication and other treatments necessary to nurse you back to health.

What comes to your mind when you think of PTSD? Do you think that Post Traumatic Stress is a Disorder only associated with war veterans? What about other high stress and dangerous professions? What would cause an ordinary civilian to experience PTSD? How is someone effected when they are diagnosed with PTSD? In other words, what kinds of symptoms or side effects do they experience?

Do you remember the tragic deadly mass shootings at Columbine High School and Sandy Hook Elementary School? What about other mass shootings that happened over the years since? Many psychologists said that those children might suffer from PTSD and because of that, counseling was made available to them because of the traumatizing experience they went through. PTSD is clinically defined as a psychiatric disorder that occurs in people who have witnessed or experienced trauma or life threatening experiences. It deals with stressful or dangerous situations that has long lasting psychological effects.

People have went off to war and seen so much carnage that they returned home never being themselves again. And all it takes is something small to trigger an episode. If we examine the definition of PTSD and compare it to what black people experience in what is called the ghetto, we will see that it fits a lot of what black people go through all our lives growing up in the ghettos of America.

Why isn't this juxtaposition done to explain and treat conditions brought on by traumatic experiences that black people face in this country? Do you think this is a stretch of the imagination? Whether it's on a battlefield, a school, or the projects, they all can cause PTSD. But for some reason we never hear of PTSD associated with black children whose neighborhoods are like warzones.

We are not talking about just an isolated incident here or there, but these types of incidents happen so frequently that they have become normalized. What does the effect of this produce in young black children? If PTSD can be attributed to being in or witnessing life threatening situations, hasn't many young black children experienced and/or been exposed to a traumatizing situations that should classify them as having PTSD? What effect does this have on a young child's brain? What kind of desensitization goes on? What triggers an episode? Even in this, there seems to be great disparity. You hear about black neighborhoods being described as warzones all the time but PTSD is never mentioned as a byproduct of that child's exposure to deadly violence.

I think children, or anyone who undergoes a traumatic experience needs adequate professional counseling to manage that experience. If not treated, the person with PTSD can experience anxiety, depression, or have anger issues. I bring this up to help explain some of the mental health issues that may come from PTSD even if we haven't been professionally diagnosed as having it.

Lastly, the matter of reparations has been a discussion for many years among a segment of the black community. And as of the date of this writing, in Evanston, Illinois, a reparations bill was passed. Now, there is a broader national discussion being had when just a few short years ago this subject wouldn't have even been entertained. And as always, there are those pushing back on the idea of reparations.

For some reason the trite tactic of putting a black face up as a voice giving reasons why he thinks it is a bad idea to give black people reparations of any kind and that the focus should be on more inclusive solutions that deal with some of the everyday problems both blacks and whites are confronted with. I'm all for a better world. I think most people are. But I don't see how giving the descendants of slaves the promise that was made to their forefathers as bad thing. I don't see how doing what is necessary to repair the damage that was done to an entire people as something that shouldn't be done.

One concern I heard is that simply giving black people financial reparations alone will do nothing but further cripple us by keeping us in a dependent state. If that is true, then it is a legitimate concern. At the same time, if that is true, isn't that further evidence of the messed up condition that we are in as a result of the long lasting effects of slavery and injustice? When you look at reparations, you have to hone in on the word repair. When you repair something that has been broken or destroyed, you do whatever it takes to bring that thing back to its original state or condition.

To undo what has been done to us is not something that can be fixed with money alone. Our entire mental, moral, and spiritual selves must be a part of the package considered for any meaningful reparations process. This includes taking a look at the systems that are currently in place and flushing them of the racial tint that is in each of them. What would forty acres and a mule be worth today? If it can be determined what today's equivalent is of what a dollar was a hundred years ago, then it can be computed to figure out today's equivalent to what forty acres and mule would be worth today.

Land is real estate. Real estate generally appreciates overtime. Not to mention what could be farmed or erected on that land. What would a mule be worth today in relation to what it's function was then? I don't have the answers to these questions, but with the minds that we have it should not be hard to calculate what would be of comparable value using the appropriate metrics.

A more excellent way in my mind would be reconciling yesterday's events with a solution that embodies today's reality. The question is, is something like that possible? Even if the original idea that undergirded this nation was one that unforeseen what this country and the world would look like centuries later; in the interest of peace, and in the interest of a better world, there needs to be a way to become more mature to embrace a loftier idea.

That would be making a more perfect union. When your principles are static and the world around you is evolving, you will write yourself out of history by making yourself irrelevant because you represent an idea that is out of season. It is written that when I was a child I spoke as a child, I understood as a child, I thought as a child; but when I became a man, I put away childish things. Let's man up, take responsibility, and move forward together in a more excellent way.

If you want to continue leading the world America, then start by setting the example of what it means to be a civilized society that ensures equal rights and equal justice under the laws of the land.

12_ Out of the Mouths of Babes

"Out of the mouth of babes and suckling has thou ordained strength because of thine enemies, that thou mightiest still the enemy and the avenger." Psalms 8:2

The primary subject matter in this chapter is taken from the words in the above verse. We will continue with the same overall theme in this chapter as the previous ones. However, here we will show you how despite the overwhelming effort by the enemy through all of the tricks, lies, discrimination, systemic racism, or any other devious or underhanded means to disrupt and dismantle any efforts made by today's social justice groups or civil rights organizations, those efforts will prove to be futile in the end.

We are living in a time when the stance being taken by the younger generation has been strengthened and backed by God. And out the mouths of babes will come strong words of wisdom of God because they have been taught by God and have been imbued and fortified with His spirit. These words will gradually produce the long-awaited world sought after. Words produce worlds.

This is a new dispensation of time. Voices are being raised at a rate and by a segment of society in record numbers. These voices transcend the color line. People from all walks of life are affected by the pervasive element of injustice that hits home almost everywhere.

This tidal wave of voices in opposition to the status quo is something that can only be attempted to be stopped through manipulating, dividing, or enticing those who want a better nation and a better world.

By manipulating I'm referring to the lie campaigns that we discussed earlier in this book that are used to discredit a movement, an individual, or a people through evil machinations that involves deliberate mischaracterizations and minimizing the need for such groups or organizations tackling social justice and race-related issues.

* Just so we're clear, mischaracterization is another word for a lie. Since all warfare is based upon deception, the first casualty of war is the truth. Winston Churchill had an interesting take on the truth. He reportedly once said that the truth is so valuable that it had to be protected by a bodyguard full of lies.

This shows just how valuable the truth is and it points to the lengths others will go to keep the truth hidden. Because of this viewpoint, nothing is off the table and nothing is beyond the scope of being done to protect lies America doesn't want exposed. This is nothing new. Just think about how many countless times have our good leaders been vilified for speaking the truth. For calling for justice? How many times have others been fearful of standing with those who speak the truth on their behalf for fear of being penalized in some way? Character assassination is a weapon used to cast anyone who attempts to expose the truth in its deadly crosshairs.

Mischaracterizations are the bodyguards that act like the assassin's bullet. It is not intended to kill the person physically. It is intended to kill the belief and confidence in the one mischaracterized and the ideas they embody. The attempt is to sever the head from the body.

Only to find out later, many years after the good leader's death, that that leader was the target of false charges and accusations to weaken their effective connection with their people. This is being done right now today with any leader or potential leader who can reach the sheeplike masses.

The forces of good and evil, and truth and falsehood have always contended with each other, and it seems that things are at a feverish pitch. This is why we need the wisdom of the elders who know the battlefield better than the younger generation to help guide them through this minefield. Otherwise, we run the risk of repeating many of the mistakes we made in the past.

Sadly and unfortunately, many of the so-called freedom fighters of yesterday, and even some of the newer ones today, have committed the most egregious act that can be committed, that of selling their people out by mortgaging the future of the youth and future generations for crumbs. This kind of double-crossing is done in the shadows outside of the public eye. Then you have those who are true to the cause, but they have simply weakened over time and lost their resolve to fight anymore. And this is why they should fade to the back and counsel the youth and teach them tactical approaches to fight injustice.

The elders are for counsel and the youth are for war.

Greed has a way of supplanting moral principles, righteous motives, and deeply held convictions. If someone can be turned so easily to travel the path of Judas to betray the trust of a people who look for and see only the good in their leaders, then we are in bad shape.

When you can sever that kind of connection through your manipulations, it makes it hard for the body to stand without its head, but the good thing is that it forces the body to grow another head for survival's sake. Divide and conquer is an age-old tactic used to weaken others so that their success will be greatly handicapped. All means, methods, and mediums are used to foment division to render those divided powerless and ineffective.

The machinations used are varied and calculated to produce a wedge between the elders and the youth. As we've said, if you cut off the head, the body will follow. This accounts for much of the disarray among the masses. We are without effective leadership. Not that we don't have effective leaders. While we do have powerful minds spearheading movements, they have to go toe to toe with the gravitational pull of things that distract the people and dull their senses. The distraction comes in the form of the entertainment industry, the sports world, and the celebration of pagan holidays.

The dulling of the senses makes us nonresponsive en masse to the call for un. This is the aim of the enemy. To keep the youth without effective leadership to lean on for guidance in these perilous and tumultuous times. The enemy understands the importance of the head. In the head is where the wisdom comes from. The direction. The cautionary advice. The provisions. We must wisely and systematically deal with the condition that we are in if it is to change.

This responsibility is ultimately on us. God will never help people change their condition unless they put forth the effort to change their own condition. The failure of the government to play a larger role in eradicating the problems that the little person suffers from is one thing, but when we fail ourselves, that's another thing. We can't afford to wait hand and foot for someone else's benevolence and goodwill.

We have tried that approach time and time again and we have always ended up with the short end of the stick. Besides, there are consequences for any person or people who rely completely on others to do for them what they can do themselves. For the mouths of babes to speak with wisdom they have to be connected to a higher power and source. Could this be why it is written in the 6th chapter of the book of Matthews, "Give us this day, our daily bread?". This daily bread is provision. Provisions are necessary for an army out on the battlefield.

Cutting off the supply lines of opposing armies from their daily rations serves to neutralize them over time. And this is why the youth need their daily rations. These daily rations are their marching orders. Their daily report on the state of the movement. We cannot afford not to have our daily bread from those who are at the forefront of change not to be delivered.

Unity is the key that unites and it unlocks the inner potential of a force designed to overcome any other force that opposes it. Wisdom is the way. Strategy is the way. Unity is the way. Courage is the way. Ignorance, emotionalism, irrationality, and fearfulness must be done away with. Much more can be accomplished collectively, in the right way, than can be done individually, in an unorganized way.

The cloak of fear has been removed and the people would rather lose everything, including their very lives, than continue to be persecuted. It is something about persecution that makes someone rather face death than the searing pain of injustice. Each of us has a tolerance level beyond which we can't or aren't willing to go beyond.

Covid has had an intangible effect on all of this as it relates to the normalization of death. Although each of us will meet death when she comes knocking on our door, when death is all around us and we face the prospect of death routinely, and we escape it, it lessens our fear of it. Speaking truth to power is not easy. It takes a certain kind of testicular fortitude to face a power structure that has the ability to squash and silence you by using only a fraction of its weight. This type of strength is hard to find because the system that we are under is also designed to emasculate men.

Throughout history, those who have been at the forefront of change have paid hefty prices. Some have even paid the ultimate sacrifice by paying with their lives for a cause they saw as bigger than themselves. Now we arrive at the Joshua generation. This is the youth. These are they who will speak and act in such a way that puts the opposition on notice and stop him in his tracks. He wonders what manner of people is this. Their crazy he says. Look at them. All of the shooting and killing. If they somehow turned against us the way they have turned on one another, we might be in trouble. So here comes the war on so-called drugs.

Remember when Pharaoh invited the others by saying, "Let us deal wisely with them, lest they latch onto an enemy of ours and come against us. So, let's get them up out the land...".
The war on gangs is on different fronts and it kills a couple of birds with one stone. If executed effectively, it can cause tribal strife or gang warfare. Which leads to death or incarceration. This is only one part of the Joshua generation.

The other Joshuans are more conscious of social issues. Their aim is not at one another. They fight against tyrannical rule. They fight for human rights. This makes them even more dangerous. They are targeted differently, yet similarly. The goal of the targeting is the same which is to render them ineffective. This is where the enticing comes in. This can be money, access, a vice, or whatever can be used to take their attention and focus away from the struggle for real liberation.

We need to keep one thing in mind, that power concedes nothing without a demand. Why should any authoritative body relinquish something if they don't have to? Especially if they think it is not in their best interest to do so. They shouldn't. And they won't.

If you and I are foolish enough to think that the concessions that we seek will be given freely without a real demand from us that we will withdraw our support, in the form of votes, dollars, or otherwise, then we won't get any of our needs and concerns met. At the same time, the leaders would be wise to recognize that a movement is brewing and it contains an element that was missing from those who in times past went to the limit of their capabilities.

Today is different. We are matching their sophistication with our own. We are matching their dissemination of information with our own. The field of play is being leveled. When this happens, the odds slowly begin to decrease in their favor and slowly begin to increase in ours. It's a shame it has come to an us versus them thing. It really is. We didn't make it this way. And many of us would rather it wasn't this way. I know I wish it wasn't. But you did this. The you and the us are not tied to color but to belief and ideology. You know who you are.

If you are not the architect behind all of this division, then you are with us. If you are not the cause or the one who perpetuates all of this color madness, I'm not talking about you. None of us today initiated any of this. But it exists, so we might as well deal with it

Many times a player either on a basketball team or a football team may foul a player on the other team overly aggressive. The player this is done to reacts just as aggressive.

But the ref didn't see the initial foul so it doesn't get called. All he sees is the retaliatory foul. The one who responded to the affront is penalized while the original wrongdoer gets off.

The ref is the media. Yet they are conscious of the facts of history. They know who the initial fouler is. The choose to ignore that and focus squarely on those who respond to being fouled.

This in turn makes it seems as we are overreaching when in fact we are not. So the less conscious of us, or the more fearful of us, shy away from being connected with anyone who rightfully defends themselves because of the aesthetics. You get the picture. Knowing this, we put forth our case to let our side be heard. Now, the jurists, which are the American people, get to decide the case. Hopefully this is done strictly upon the strength of our arguments, the merits, and the strong evidence presented. And if the jury is fair and impartial, and we present a strong case, then they will come back with a guilty verdict for America on all counts.

This is what I have attempted to do in this book. To present arguments. Facts. Evidence. With the hopes that it will help those who are completely unaware and blind to what happened historically between the races. I am a novice writer. So excuse me for any mistake I may have made or for any unintelligent proposition I put forth.

Again, as I close, I want to remind the readers that I'm not a college graduate. I'm not even a high school graduate. I don't possess any technical expertise in any given area. But I have committed myself to learning, howbeit, unconventionally.

My views reflect my condition and circumstances. As objective as I have tried to be, there was no way subjective elements could have been avoided. I have been in prison going on thirty two years. I blame no one for me being here. At the same time, this experience has afforded me a unique perspective. I don't apologize for that. Others whose condition and circumstances are different have different perspectives. And I respect that.

I am a firm believer in all things working together for good to them that love God, to them who are called according to his purpose. I can't fully say I know what my purpose is. All I know is that I've had a lot of time to reflect over my life and life in general. I have missed great opportunities that would have caused my life to turn out much differently. But, for some reason, here I am. And I have no complaints. I will end this little book with by paying a special homage in the next chapter.

13 _The Unforgotten

I think that it is only right that we conclude this book by mentioning the many names of those who are the primary reason why this book is being written. The names of the men and women below lost their lives by the hands of police, a vigilante wannabe, or some lunatic. Although the circumstances are different in every encounter, the end results were all the same, ending in the death of a black man or black woman. In our fight for social justice and better race relations, We can't afford to let their deaths be in vain.

These lives, although they ended tragically, will live on in the hearts and minds of those who will use their loss as fuel to bring about the change necessary to end these types of incidents. The torchlight that we carry to fight for justice is on your behalf and in all of your names. Your memories will live on. You will never be forgotten.

I know this list is not exhaustive so please excuse me if a name is mistakenly omitted. Contact us so that any missed names can be added to future printings. Only names, ages, and when and where these killings took place will be listed.

THE HAND THAT ROCKS THE CRADLE

Nicholas Hey ward Jr., 13; New York, NY – 8/ 27/ 1994

James Byrd, 49; Jasper, TX – 6/ 7/ 1998

Amadou Diallo, 23; Bronx, NY – 2/ 4/ 1999

Ricky Byrdsong, 34; Skokie, IL – 7/ 3/ 1999

Anthony Dwain Lee, 39; Los Angeles, CA –10/ 28/ 2000

Alberta Sprull, 57; New York, NY – 5/16/ 2003

Timothy Stansbury Jr., 19; New York, NY – 1/ 24/ 2004

Kathryn Johnston, 92; Atlanta, GA – 11/ 21/ 2006

Sean Bell, 23; Queens, NY – 11/ 25/ 2006

Deaunta Farrow, 12; West Memphis, AR – 6/ 22/ 2007

Marvin Parker, 52; Kansas City, MO – 9/ 7/ 2008

Julian Alexander, 20; Anaheim, CA – 10/ 29 2008

Oscar Grant, 22; Oakland, CA – 1/ 1/ 2009

Lawrence Allen, 20; Philadelphia, PA – 2/ 20/ 2009

Aiyana Stanley-Jones, 7; Detroit, MI - 5/ 16/ 2010

Danroy "DJ" Henry Jr., 20; Thornwood, N –10/ 17/2010

Eugene Ellison, 67; Little Rock, AR – 12/9/ 2010

Robert Ricks, 23; Alexandria, LA – 2/ 6/ 2011

Cletis Williams, 57; Jonesboro, AR – 10/ 31/ 2011

Kenneth Chamberlain Sr., 66;White Plains, NY11/19/ 11

Willie Ray Banks, 52; Granite Shoals, TX -12/ 29/ 2011

Trayvon Martin, 17; Miami, FL – 2/ 5/ 2012

Rekia Boyd, 22; Chicago, IL – 3/ 21/ 2012

Darius Simmons, 13; Milwaukee, WI – 5/ 31/ 2012

Sgt. James Brown, 26; El Paso, TX – 7/15/ 2012

Mohamed Bah, 28; New York, NY – 9/25/ 2012

Jordan Davis, 17; Jacksonville, FL – 11/ 23/ 2012

Darnesha Harris, 17; Breaux Bridge, LA – 12/ 2/ 2012

Corey Stingley, 16; Milwaukee, WI – 12/ 29/ 2012

Kayla Moore, 41; Berkeley, CA – 2/ 12/ 2013

Kimani Gray, 16; Brooklyn, NY – 3/10/ 2013

Wayne A. Jones, 50; Martinsburg, WV -3/ 13/ 2013

Gabriel Winzer, 25; Kaufman County, TX -4/ 27/ 2013

Deion Fludd, 17; New York, NY – 7/ 12/ 2013

Jonathan Ferrel , 24; Charlotte, NC – 9/ 14/ 2013

Renisha McBride, 19; Dearborn Hts, MI – 11/ 2/ 2013

Yvette Smith, 47; Bastrop, TX – 2/ 16/ 2014

Marquise Jones, 23; San Antonio, TX – 2/ 28/ 2014

Victor White III, 22; New Iberia, LA -3/ 3/ 2014

Jerry Dwight Brown, 41; Zephyrhills, FL -7/ 1/ 2014

Eric Garner, 43; Staten Island, NY – 7/17/ 2014

John Crawford III, 22; Beavercreek, OH – 8/ 5/ 2014

Amir Brooks, 17; Washington, D.C. -8/ 6/2014

Ezell Ford, 25; Los Angeles, CA - 8 11/ 2014

Dante Parker, 36; Victorville, CA – 8/12/ 2014

Michelle Cusseaux, 50; Phoenix, AZ – 8/14/ 2014

Kajieme Powell, 25; St. Louis, MO – 8/ 19,/2014

Michael Brown, 18; Ferguson, MO – 9/ 8/2014

Darrien Hunt, 22; Saratoga Springs, UT – 9/ 12014

Cameron Tillman, 14; Houma, LA – 9/23, 2014

Laquan McDonald, 17; Chicago, IL – 10/20/ 2014

Tanisha Anderson, 37; Cleveland, OH - 13 / 2014

Akai Hurley, 28; Brooklyn, NY – 11/20/ 2014

Tamir Rice, 12; Cleveland, OH -11/ 22/ 2014

Rumain Brisbon, 34; Phoenix, AZ – 12/ 4/ 2014

Natasha McKenna, 37; Alexandria, VA -2/ 7/ 2015

Walter Scott, 50; North Charleston, SC -4/4/ 2015

Norman Cooper, 33; San Antonio, TX – 4/ 19/ 2015

Freddie Gray, 25; Baltimore, MD – 4/ 19/ 2015

Kalief Browder, 22; Bronx, NY – 6/ 6/ 2015

Tywanza Sanders, 26; Charleston, SC – 6/17/ 2015

Clementa Pinckney, 41; Charleston, SC -6/ 17/ 2015

Sharonda C-Singleton, 45; Charleston, SC-6/ 17/ 2015

Depayne M-Doctor, 49; Charleston, SC -6/ 17/ 2015

Cynthia Hurd, 54; Charleston, SC – 6/17/ 2015

Myra Thompson, 59; Charleston, SC -6/ 17/ 2015

Ethel Lance, 70; Charleston, SC -6/ 17/ 2015

Daniel Simmons, 74; Charleston, SC - 6/ 17/ 2015

Susie Jackson, 87; Charleston, SC - 6/ 17/ 2015

Sandra Bland, 28; Hempstead, TX – 7/13/ 2015

Darrius Stewart, 19; Memphis, TN – 7/17/ 2015

Samuel Dubose, 43; Cincinnati, OH – 7/ 19/ 2015

Corey Jones, 31; Boynton Beach, FL -10/ 18/ 2015

Quintonio Legrier, 19; Chicago, IL – 12/ 26/ 2015

Bettie Jones, 55; Chicago, IL – 12/ 26/ 2015

Antronie Scott, 36; San Antonio, TX – 2/ 4/ 2016

David Joseph, 17; Austin, TX – 2/ 8/ 2016

Jay Anderson Jr., 25; Wauwatosa, WI – 6/ 23/ 2016 Alton Sterling, 37;

Baton Rouge, LA -7/ 5/ 2016

Philando Castile, 32; Falcon Heights, MN – 7/ 6/ 2016

Joseph Mann, 51; Sacramento, CA – 7/ 11/ 2016

Donnell Thompson Jr., 27; Compton, CA -7/ 28/ 2016

Jamarion Robinson, 26; East Point, GA -8/ 5/ 2016

Christian Taylor, 19; Fort Worth, TX – 8/7/ 2016

Terrence Crutcher, 40; Tulsa, OK – 9/ 16/ 2016

Alfred Olango, 38; El Cajon, CA – 9/ 27/ 2016

Deborah Danner, 66; New York, NY – 10/ 18/ 2016

Desmond Phillips, 25; Chico, CA – 3/17/ 2017

Alteria Woods, 21; Gifford, FL – 3/19/ 2017

Timothy Caughman, 66; Manhattan, NY -3/20/ 2017

Jordan Edwards, 15; Balch Springs, TX – 4/ 29/ 2017

Mikel McIntyre, 32; Ranch Cordova, CA – 5/ 8/ 2017

Charleena Lyles, 30; Seattle, WA – 6/ 18/ 2017

James Lacy, 47; San Diego, CA – 8/ 7/ 2017

Damon Grimes, 15; Detroit, MI – 8/ 26/ 2017

Antwaine Williams Jr., 19; Inkster, MI – 11/ 2/ 2017

Ronell Foster, 33; Vajello, CA – 2/ 13/ 2018

Stephon Clark, 23; Sacramento, CA -3/ 18/ 2018

. Danny Ray Thomas, 34; Houston, TX – 3/ 22/ 2018

Dorian Harris, 17; Memphis, TN – 3/ 29/ 2018

Marcus-David Peters, 24; Richmond, VA -5/ 14/ 2018

Earl McNeil, 40; National City, CA -5/ 26/ 2018

Robert White, 41; Silver Spring, MD – 6/16/ 2018

Antwon Rose Jr., 17; Pittsburgh, PA – 6/19/ 2018

Jason Washington, 45; Portland, OR – 6/ 29/ 2018

Harith Augustus, 37; Chicago, IL – 7/ 14/ 2018

Botham Jean, 26, Dallas, TX – 9/ 6/ 2018

Charles Roundtree Jr.18; San Antonio, TX –10/ 17/2018

Jemel Roberson, 26; Robbins, IL – 11/ 11/ 2018

Emantic Bradford Jr., 21; Hoover, AL – 11/22/ 2018

Aleah Jenkins, 24; La Jolla, CA – 11/ 27/ 2018

Jasmine McBride, 30; Flint, MI – 2/ 12/ 2019

Bradley Blackshire, 30; Little Rock AR -2/ 22/ 2019

Sterling Higgins, 37; Union City, TN – 3/ 24/ 2019

Ronald Greene, 49; Union Parish, LA – 5/10/ 2019

Pamela Turner, 44; Baytown, TX – 5/ 13/ 2019

Dominique Clayton, 32; Oxford, MS -5/ 19/ 2019

Titi "Tete" Gulley, 31; Portland, OR -5/ 27/ 2019

Jaleel Medlock, 21; Conway, AR – 7/ 16/ 2019

. Elijah McClain, 23; Aurora, CO -8/ 30/ 2019

Byron Williams, 50; Las Vegas, NV -9/ 5/ 2019

Atatiana Jefferson, 28; Fort Worth, TX – 10/ 12/ 2019

Michael Dean, 28; Temple, TX – 12/ 2/ 2019

John Neville, 56; Winston-Salem, NC – 12/ 4/ 2019

Miciah Lee, 18; Sparks, NV – 1/ 5/ 2020

Darius Tarver, 23; Denton, TX – 1/ 23/ 2020

William Green, 43; Temple Hills, MD – 1/ 27/ 2020

Jaquyn O'Neill Light, 20; Graham, NC-1/28/2020

Lionel Morris, 39; Conway, AR – 2/ 4/ 2020

Ahmaud Arbery, 25; Satilla Shores, GA – 2/ 23/ 2020

Manuel Ellis, 33; Tacoma, WA -3/ 3/ 2020

Barry Gedeus, 27; Fort Lauderdale, FL – 3/ 8/ 2020

Breonna Taylor, 26; Louisville, KY – 3/ 13/ 2020

Daniel Prude, 30; Rochester, NY – 3/30/ 2020

Steven Taylor, 33; San Leandro, CA – 4/ 18/ 2020

Cornelius Fredericks, 16; Kalamazoo, MI -5/ 1/ 2020

Maurice Gordon, 28; Bass River, NJ – 5/ 23/ 2020

George Floyd, 46; Minneapolis, MN -5/ 25/ 2020

Dion Johnson, 28; Phoenix, AZ -5/ 25/ 2020

Tony McDade, 38; Tallahassee, FL.-5/ 27/ 2020

Calvin Horton Jr., 43; Minneapolis, MN -5/ 27/ 2020

James Scurlock, 22; Omaha, NE – 5/ 30/ 2020

David McAtee, 53; Louisville, KY – 6/ 1/ 2020

Jamel Floyd, 35; New York, NY -6/ 3/ 2020

Kamal Flowers, 24; New Rochelle, NY – 6/ 5/ 2020

Robert Forbes, 56; Bakersfield, CA - June 6, 2020

Priscilla Slater, 38; Harper Woods, MI – 6/ 10/ 2020

Rayshard Brooks, 27; Atlanta, GA – 6/ 12/ 2020

Maurice Abisdid-Wagner, 30; Maui, HI – 7/ 26/ 2020

Julian Lewis, 60; Sylvania, GA – 8/ 7/ 2020

Anthony McClain, 32; Pasadena, CA – 8/ 15/ 2020

Damian Daniels, 30; San Antonio, TX – 8/ 25/ 2020

Dijon Kizzee, 29; Los Angeles, CA – 8/ 31/ 2020

Kurt Reinhold, 42; San Clemente, CA – 9/ 23/ 2020

Jonathan Price, 31; Wolfe City, TX – 10/ 3/ 2020

Walter Wallace Jr., 27; Philadelphia, PA – 10/ 26/ 2020

Kevin Peterson Jr., 21; Vancouver, WA – 10/ 29/ 2020

Quawan Charles, 15; Iberia Parish, LA – 11/ 3/ 2020

Aiden Ellison, 19; Ashland, OR – 11/ 23/ 2020

Casey Goodson Jr., 23; Columbus, OH – 12/ 4/ 2020

Bennie Edwards, 60; Oklahoma City, OK –12/ 11/ 2020

Vincent Belmonte, 18; Cleveland, OH – 1/ 5/ 2021

Robert Howard, 30; Memphis, TN – 1/5/ 2021

Xzavier Hill, 18; Goochland County, VA - 1/ 9/ 2021

Patrick Warren, 52; Killeen, TX – 1/ 10/ 2021

Jenoah Donald, 30; Hazel Dell, WA – 2/ 9/ 2021

Marvin Scott III, 26; McKinney, TX – 3/14/ 2021

Dominique Williams, 32; Takoma Park, MD -4/ 7/ 2021

James Lionel Johnson, 38; Takoma Park, MD -4/ 7,/21 Daunte Wright, 20; Brooklyn Center, MN -4/ 12/ 2021

Matthew"Zadok" Williams, 35; DeKalb, GA -4/ 12/ 2021 Adam Toledo, 13 ; Chicago, IL – 4/ 2021

Andrew Brown Jr., ; Elizabeth City, NC – 4/ 21/ 2021

Shereese Francis, 29; New York – 2012

Ma'Khia Bryant, 16; Columbus, OH. -4/ 2021

Tyrea Pryor, 39; Independence, MO – 3/ 11/ 2022

Malcolm Trieste Staton, 30; Monroe, NC – 3/ 15/ 2022

Rodney K. Robinson II, 21; Dewey Beach Del.3/19/22

Robert L. Wright, 34; Aiken S.C. -4/7, 2022

Paul Derrick Moss II, 51; Knox County Tenn 8/14/2022

Alonzo Nesby, 60; Huber Heights Ohio -8/14,2022 Andrew Tekle Sundberg 20; Minneapolis, Minn. 7/13/22 Jaiden Malik Carter 19; Woodbridge, VA – 9/ 1/ 2022

Derrick Ameer Ellis-Cook, Burien, Wash. – 9/9/ 2022 Jaylen Lewis, 25; Jackson, Miss. – 9/ 25/ 2022

Christopher L. Ardoin, 31; Lake Charles, LA 10/1/2022 Immanueal J. C-Johnson, 30; Portland, Ore.11/ 19/22 Timothy McCree Johnson, 37; Fairfax VA – 2/ 22/ 2023

James Lanier, 34; Wallace N.C. – 2/ 24/2023

Alonzo Sentell Bagley, 43; Shreveport LA – 3/ 3/ 2023 Odell Hicks Jr., 51; Harrison County Texas – 3/ 23 2023

Jamarr V-T Thompson, 40; Houston Texas –4/ 11/ 23 Amaree'ya Henderson, 25; Kansas City, Kan –4/ 26/23 Lance Lockett, 41; El Dorado, ARK – 5/ 2/ 2023

Calvin Cains III, 18; Metairie LA – 6/ 6/ 2023

Jordan Richardson, 18; Rantoul ILL – 6/ 7/ 2023 Marcell T. Nelson, 42; Kansas City, MO – 6/ 9/ 2023 Jarveon Hudspeth, 21; Memphis Tenn. – 6/24/ 2023

Randy A. Jackson, 39; Champaign County, ILL –7/ 3/23

Jarrell Garris, 37; New Rochelle N.Y. – 7/ 3/ 2023

Ahmad Abdullah, 25; Huntington W. Virginia –7/ 3/23

PoniaX Kane Calles, 33; Greham Ore. – 7/ 22/ 2023

Tahiem Weeks-Cook, 22; Philadelphia PA – 8/4/2023

Brandon Cole, 36; Denver Colorado – 8/ 5/ 2023

Xavier Bejamine Lacosta, 31; San Diego CA – 8/ 15/ 23

Tahman Kenneth Wilson, 20; Marinez, CA – 8/ 18/ 2023 Lueth MO, 15; Syracuse NY – 9/ 6/ 2023

Lamoris D. Speight Jr., 22; Saratoga N.C. – 9/10/ 2023

Sterlin Keyon Arnold, 43; Huntsville Ala. – 9/ 14/ 2023

. Emmanual Millard, 20; Roswell GA – 10/ 12/ 2023

Leonard Cure, 53; Camden County GA – 10/16/ 2023

Darcel Edwards, 35; Indianapolis, Indiana –10/24/23

Demarcus Brodie, 49; Fayetteville N.C. –11/ 23/ 2023

Michael Antonio Codo Jr., 23; Griffin GA – 12/10/2023

Tony Cox, 33; Pontiac MI, 12/13/ 2023

Peyton Lawrence, 19; Mesquite, Texas – 12/ 14/ 2023

Jonathan Bady, 31; Raleigh, Tenn. – 12/21/ 2023

Vaughn Malloy, Stonington Conn. – 12/21/ 2023

Victor Figueroa Roblero, 48; Spartanburg, S.C. 1/ 1/24

Roshod Graham, 30; Lauderhill Fla. – 2/ 2/ 2024

Issac Goodlaw III, 30; Carol Stream ILL. - 2/ 3/ 2024

Phillip Austin Brant, 26; Manassas, VA – 2/ 13/ 2024

Marvin Martin III, 50; Chillicothe – 2/ 13/ 2024

THE HAND THAT ROCKS THE CRADLE

William Lowery, 46; Sheriden Wyoming – 2/14/ 2024

Conclusion

The Hand that Rocks the Cradle refers to, as we have shown, the earliest part of someone's life or any point of origin of a thing that exercises the greatest influence or control in someone's life. We have attempted to highlight those systems that we believe played and continue to play a pivotal role in society's social condition and racial upheaval. I may not have given the most comprehensive arguments that relate to every social and racial issue there is. However, this book deals with social justice issues and race relations in a way that separates them from traditional norms. Unless we take a serious hard honest look at some of the primal and hidden causes of the problems in society when it comes to social justice issues and race relations, then it will always be like playing a game of hide and seek. We will always be looking for justice but won't ever be able to find it.

Black people have been subjected to some of the worst treatment that any people have ever had to experience. For some reason, many people try to sweep this fact under the rug as if what went on yesterday has no bearing on what is going today. But we know that the effects of that treatment has undeniably caused the destruction of the black family unit, produced self-hatred, has us in financial ruins, and has caused a slew of other problems. I am not making excuses or absolving ourselves of the responsibility to change our own condition, but the facts are the facts.

Somehow we know our condition involves more than what we can explain, but we can't quite put our finger on it. We have always been able to intuitively understand something greater than our ability to put what we understand or feel into words. I hope that The Hand that Rocks the Cradle has supplied some of those words or explanations that gives clarity to what you already knew but couldn't find the right words to explain when it comes to social justice and race relations.

It is difficult to speak in depth about anything if you haven't experienced it firsthand. And equally difficult, if not more, to understand anything for the same reason. However, when someone writes or speaks about something that you struggle to understand or agree with because your life's experiences have been so vastly different, then at least give those whose views are different than yours a degree of latitude. Instead of judging, being dismissive, or being offended, try to understand why someone else thinks, feels, or sees things the way they do.

By doing this it may not bring you into agreement or make it any easier to swallow, but at least you may be better able to understand another's perspective that differs from your own.

Any form of discrimination based upon someone's race, class, or belief is unacceptable. Yet this is the reality that people have to deal with daily. The writer of this book has been a recipient of the things that has caused him to explore the far reaching and penetrating views expressed in this book. Views that he knows will elicit a broad reaction. Nevertheless, he feels strongly about his expressed sentiments and desires not to foment dissention or to further fan the flames of division, but wants to put honest dialogue on the table for meaningful discussion.

The one thing we cannot afford to do is rely on the government to bear the full responsibility of what we can do. All we need is the desire, the commitment, and the unity to do something about the things we want to see changed. Yes, the government has a role to play to help facilitate this change, but we who are the most affected should use our dissatisfaction to produce the change we so desperately desire.

No one will ever be able to know your pain, your suffering, or your hurt the way you do. And when someone does not have that kind of relatability, then they will not be as inclined to help in an area they have no direct or personal connection to. This is why it is on us. People champion causes for many reasons. And no reason is more personal than having your life directly impacted in some way by the cause you take up.

So, the real and most effective solutions are going to come from those who have been impacted the most. As long as the hand continues to rock the cradle, then that person or those people will continue to rule the world.

Terry Triggs

THE HAND THAT ROCKS THE CRADLE

Other Works From The Author

The Master's Deck I

The Master's Deck II

The Master's Deck III

Dark Nights and Cold Winters

The Blue Print

Made in the USA
Columbia, SC
15 July 2024

38463080R00107